COMPETITION
IN
GOVERNMENT-FINANCED
SERVICES

COMPETITION IN GOVERNMENT-FINANCED SERVICES

JOHN C. HILKE

QUORUM BOOKS
New York • Westport, Connecticut • London

Library of Congress Cataloging-in-Publication Data

Hilke, John C.
    Competition in government-financed services / John C. Hilke.
        p.   cm.
    Includes bibliographical references and index.
    ISBN 0-89930-750-7 (alk. paper)
    1. Privatization—United States.   2. Contracting out—United
States.   3. Competition—United States.   I. Title.
    HD3888.H55   1992
    338.973—dc20   91-36409

British Library Cataloguing in Publication Data is available.

Library of Congress Catalog Card Number: 91-36409
ISBN: 0-89930-750-7

First published in 1992

Quorum Books, One Madison Avenue, New York, NY 10010
An imprint of Greenwood Publishing Group, Inc.

Printed in the United States of America

∞™

The paper used in this book complies with the
Permanent Paper Standard issued by the National
Information Standards Organization (Z39.48-1984).

10 9 8 7 6 5 4 3 2 1

Contents

CONTENTS

Tables and Figures

TABLES

FIGURES

Preface

This study first reviews the rationale for government financing and provision of services and presents arguments for the position that competitive provision of some of these services is likely to be more efficient. The study then examines the principal methods of increasing competition in government-financed services and presents a summary of U.S. and other industrialized countries' experiences to date in the "experiment" of increasing competition in these services. The purpose is to alert the public to the potential magnitude of cost savings from additional increases in competition in government-financed services in the United States and to describe the types of services for which increased competition is likely to be most effective in reducing costs. The insights from this review should have application to considerations of privatization in Eastern Europe and developing countries, as well as to further competitivization of government-financed services in the United States.

The author wishes to acknowledge the help and encouragement of various present and past Federal Trade Commission (FTC) staff members including Mark Frankena, James Langenfeld, John Woodbury, Curtis Wagner, Paul Pautler, and John Peterman. Appreciation is also due to Douglas Adie from Ohio State University, R. Mark Musell from the Congressional Budget Office, and various officials from the Office of Privatization at Office of Management and Budget for helpful comments and suggestions on early drafts.

Although the author holds the position of staff economist in the Bureau of Economics at the FTC, this study has not been reviewed by, nor does it necessarily reflect the views of, the Federal Trade Commission or of any individual commissioner.

1

Introduction

CONTEXT AND PURPOSE OF THE STUDY

This study primarily concerns the extent to which real resources can be saved by increasing competition in the supply of commercial services currently produced on a sole-source basis by government. The focus is on services that will continue to be financed by government even if government no longer directly produces the service.

When economists are asked about the institutional setting for voluntary exchange that typically advances the interests of consumers, the response is almost invariably a competitive setting, in which informed buyers have a choice from among several sellers. The rationale for this response is that, in the absence of market failures, a competitive setting offers the best chance of avoiding artificially high prices and shoddy services or products. Competing sellers have strong profit incentives to minimize costs for any given quality and to offer consumers the highest quality for any given price in order to gain and retain customers. Without the spur of competition, monopoly suppliers, whether public or private, may be tempted to charge excessive prices, allow quality to deteriorate, fail to minimize costs, and tolerate stagnant productivity.

Despite near unanimity about the benefits of competition to buyers, most governments, by reason of habit or law, have produced most services provided to their citizens using a sole-source supplier: the in-house agency or bureau assigned to that particular service. Until recently, economists have not contributed much to assessing the costs of sole-source internal (i.e., in-house) supply of government services, principally because economists often have associated government responsibility for *financing* (or arranging) a service, with actual government *production* of that service.[1] In fact, there is no necessary conceptual connection between the two.[2]

The traditional rationale for government involvement in financing services concerns the concept of public services. However, governments often internally produce both public and private services.[3]

Public services have distinctive characteristics that make it unlikely that private sellers will provide them in sufficient quantities to efficiently satisfy total demand.[4] In particular, public services are characterized by "nonrival consumption." The consumption of the same service by one individual does not necessarily prevent or diminish consumption by others. Public services may also be characterized by high costs of excluding would-be consumers. That is, it is costly to prevent those who have not paid for the service from consuming it, once the service has been provided to some consumers. Because of these two characteristics, it is difficult to obtain a price from consumers that is sufficient to recoup the costs of providing the public service. Each consumer will bear only a small fraction of the cost of providing the service. Thus, each consumer has an incentive to understate how much the service is worth to him or her because the amount each person consumes is largely independent of the amount he or she contributes.[5]

Government may be able to overcome this market failure by forcing consumers to reveal their valuations of different levels of public goods through the combination of voting and involuntary payments (taxes).[6] In voting, consumers are faced with choices among budget proposals that specify prices in terms of the consumers' required tax payments. By overcoming the ability of other consumers to free ride, the voting and tax combination available to governments encourages consumers to express their real valuations and may help to create a market reflecting them. In this way, the government, at least in theory, can set the level of production at the economically efficient level and obtain (purchase) that quantity of output from private producers.[7]

An example of a public service might be the broadcast of regional weather information for the Chesapeake Bay. This service involves nonrival consumption because providing the information to one person does not appreciably diminish the value of the information to others. It also presents an excludability problem because it would be difficult to broadcast to those who pay for such a service while excluding others, without resorting to expensive specialized broadcast and receiving equipment.

Private services include all services that are not public services, although they may be used as inputs in the production of public services. Private services are characterized by exclusive consumption and the ready ability of sellers to distinguish between (and exclude) those who do and do not pay.

In-house government *production*, as distinguished from *public services*, simply means that the government that finances provision of the service actually produces the service. In-house production means that this government unit hires workers, owns machinery, buys raw materials and semifinished goods, and transforms them into services. Outside *production*, as opposed to *private services*, means only that an organization other than the government that financed it produced the service. Any organization, even a different government, could, in effect, be a outside producer in this context.

Although outside production can be widely applied to many government financed products and services, there are some services for which outside production is generally held to be inappropriate. These *inherently governmental services* involve wide government discretion and extensive value judgments. Use of police powers, judicial decisions, regulation, and policy setting are among the arenas where outside production is likely to have limited applicability. Extension of market competition to inherently governmental services may encounter transactions costs and other problems such as delegation of powers and conflicts of interest. For example, delegation of the government's authority to determine guilt or innocence could be subject to abuses that would erode fundamental constitutional rights. In addition, such abuses could be very costly for the government to detect and document.[8]

Other forms of competition may be viable routes for reducing costs where outside production by private firms or other private groups is inappropriate. Both competition between agencies within a jurisdiction and competition from other governments are possible alternatives.[9]

In contrast to inherently governmental services, *commercial services* currently produced by the government are often supplied by private firms in other contexts and characterized by readily definable outputs and well-understood technologies. These services are generally good candidates for outside production aimed at reducing costs. The distinctions between commercial and inherently governmental services are not absolute; commercial services are services that are provided by the private sector for the private sector and that can also be provided by the private sector for government.

Figure 1.1 shows the distinctive combinations of production of government financed services in the format of a two-by-two table.[10] The vertical axis distinguishes between in-house and outside production. The horizontal axis distinguished between public and private services. Commercial services include all private services and those public services that are not inherently governmental services.

"Commercial public service" is not a contradiction is terms because there are some public services that are frequently provided in the private sector, but for only a segment of the citizens. For example, library services are often considered to involve nonrival consumption and positive externalities and therefore may qualify as a public service. Library services are not, however, confined to the public sector. Most major firms, for example, have libraries and so library services are a commercial service, although arguably a public service. Thus it may be possible for localities to finance more efficient outside production of library services, that is to shift production of library services from cell I to cell III. This flexibility is possible because (1) library services generally do not involve wide discretion and value judgments that make them an inherently governmental service and (2) private suppliers may be available to provide library services to the government because library services are extensively produced in the private sector.

As another example of how Figure 1.1 represents type of service and production differences, consider the Chesapeake Bay weather forecasting service example mentioned earlier. Assume initially that the service was financed by the federal government, produced in-house by the National Weather Service, and broadcast by the Coast Guard. This would make it a cell I service, although it still might be a commercial service since private firms also routinely provide both weather forecasting and broadcasting services. If instead, the government competitively contracted a private firm to both forecast and broadcast the information, the service would move from cell I to cell III because it would shift from in-house to outside production.[11]

Finally, consider a decision to put the broadcast portion of the original weather service up for bid. If the Coast Guard won the bidding, but at a lower cost than it previously experienced, the broadcast service would remain in cell I, but subject to the competitive effects of the possibility of moving to cell III.

Any type of service can be produced by the government. At the extreme, government can control virtually all means of production, as in a totalitarian communist society.[12]

Figure 1.1
Production Options for Public and Private Services
Financed by Government

	Public Services	Private Services
In-House Production	Cell I	Cell II
Outside Production	Cell III	Cell IV

At the other extreme, government can contract with private firms for production of most services, as some local governments do.[13] Finally, some public (private) services financed by a government may be supplied by a mix of in-house and outside production. This case would lie in between cells I and III (cells II and IV).

Although empirical estimates of cost savings generally include all types of cost savings,[14] this study primarily concerns ways of conserving real resources by increasing competition in the production of services in cells I and II in Figure 1.1.[15]

Despite the absence of any compelling efficiency justification for government financing or production in cell II, some governments may reject shedding these services for noneconomic reasons, and yet they may wish to supply these (cell II) services more efficiently.[16] Consequently, this study asks whether governments can increase efficiency by increasing competition in the services, particularly commercial services, that governments currently produce.[17]

In addition to real resource savings, increased competition may also reduce economic rents (i.e., wage premiums) obtained by some factors of production. Economic rents may be largely a matter of income distribution and therefore may not directly present an issue of economic efficiency (real resource savings). Appendix A provides a discussion of this distinction and chapter 4 presents empirical evidence separating direct efficiency (real resource) effects from wage premium effects. An indirect economic efficiency rationale for concern about wage premiums is that they may induce waste of real resources.[18] Wage premiums become a matter of economic efficiency concern if (1) real resources are lost in the process of raising tax revenue to finance the service, (2) real resources are consumed in preserving or enhancing the wage premiums, and (3) allocative efficiency is reduced by the distortions (in government choices about the quantity, quality, and mix of services that are supplied through government) caused by the wage premiums. Because of the possible indirect efficiency costs of wage premiums, the final empirical cost savings estimates in chapter 5 will be present estimates of both total cost savings and cost savings from direct efficiency improvements.

To anticipate the study's conclusions, sole-source in-house production of government financed services does not appear to be inevitable. Competition from various alternative sources can be introduced. Increasing competition in producing government services can both directly improve efficiency and reduce the total costs of government services at the federal, state, and local levels. This study gathers the available data to reach an overall assessment of the potential direct efficiency and total cost savings from increasing competition ("competitivization") in government-financed services that are currently produced in-house.

DETERMINING THE KINDS OF SERVICES SUITABLE FOR COMPETITION FROM OUTSIDE PRODUCERS

Whether a service is produced most efficiently by the government that finances it or by external parties can be analyzed using the same models that explain private firms' choices on the extent of various forms of vertical integration.[19] Private decisions about vertical integration are typically driven by the goal of minimizing costs. The economic literature that focuses on the comparative costs of transactions between and within organizations is termed "micro-microeconomics" or the "new institutional economics."[20] The theme of this literature is that arms-length market transactions, while ideally more efficient, are sometimes subject to various types of market failures that may make vertical integration preferable. Essentially it sometimes is too costly to obtain enough accurate information to make independent market transactions (including long-term and short-term contracts) work properly.[21]

For example, the electronics industry has found that the probability of success with consumers is greatly enhanced if marketing personnel are closely involved in developing new product designs and components. Arranging for such close contact between marketers and product developers through a contract has proven costly and difficult. Security and prospective patent rights, in particular, are difficult to specify and enforce through a prenegotiated contract. As a result, many electronics firms produce both marketing services and product development services in-house.[22]

The U.S. automobile industry in the first three quarters of the century illustrates another set of explanations for vertical integration. Although U.S. automobile manufacturing firms could have limited their efforts to assembling parts produced by independent suppliers,[23] uncertainty about supplies and uncertainty about the competitiveness of prices charged by suppliers apparently led U.S. automobile manufacturers to vertically integrate in many areas.[24] In some cases, the integration extended to the raw materials stage, as in Ford Motor Company's steel operations.[25] Integration of car body and other assembly operations also reportedly occurred for the same reasons.[26]

The problems noted above can occur within any organization, public or private. Controls within an organization may or not be able to overcome these problems better than market transactions and may add significant costs in the process.[27] The trick for both the private and public decision makers interested in minimizing costs is to determine when market failures make in-house production more efficient than buying from outside firms in a competitive market.[28]

The vertical integration literature indicates that outside production (purchasing on the open market) is routinely used by private firms to obtain many, if not most, inputs into final production of goods and services. Firms generally revert to in-house production only when there are important market failures. The market is likely to be a more efficient form of procuring inputs unless (1) there are very few potential suppliers, (2) costs of switching from one producer to another are high, (3) information about the production process and supplier performance is expensive to obtain, and (4) the good or service being provided cannot be clearly defined. Inability to institute incentives and controls in in-house government production also increases the probability that relying on the open market is the most efficient means of procuring production inputs.[29]

Many of the distinctions in product and production characteristics that are critical to decisions about vertical integration parallel the discussion of product characteristics in the product quality literature.[30] For example, "inspection" services in that literature are defined as services whose quality is obvious on inspection. Inspection services often approximate the characteristics, discussed above, that are most conducive to outside production. "Experience" services require extended use to ascertain quality. Experience services involve more costly information and thus entail more difficulties in arranging efficient outside production than would be the case with inspection services. With "credence" services, quality is difficult or impossible to assess even over time, so quality tends to be assessed by monitoring inputs. The production of credence services most closely corresponds to an inherently governmental service and is therefore the most likely candidate for in-house production by the government. For example, quality of the judicial system is difficult to assess directly, but some assurance about the quality of the system is obtained by enforcing specific procedures and requiring advanced training of those who operate the system.[31]

Although the product quality literature generally supports the initial ex ante distinctions between different services that could drive producers (or even consumers) to self-manufacture,[32] this literature suggests that many consumer problems with experience services can be solved through the accumulation of information about performance of particular suppliers and through market signalling or bonding devices. Through accumulation of this type of information, consumers may find a reasonable basis for choice between individual offers of experience services. When consumers shift their purchases in response to experience, it creates incentives for firms to seek to establish a reputation for quality even in these noninspection services.[33] It seems reasonable to expect that for services that are purchased frequently in significant quantities, governments can take advantage of learning and reputation effects as well.[34] This should allow governments to expand the boundary (beyond the limited realm of inspection services) of their services that can successfully be provided by outside producers.

Although reputation effects may permit expansion of the list of government services that can be reasonably considered for outside production, quality uncertainty remains a major problem with some services financed by government. Credence services, where procedures and specific, but difficult to monitor, inputs are the primary available indicia of quality, may remain in-house government services. For such services, the advantage of outside production, the ability to identify and implement innovative combinations of inputs in production, may be outweighed by the costs (e.g., opportunities for misappropriation and conflicts of interest) or may not provide any observable advantages. Hence, there is less likely to be an observable efficiency advantage from outside production.

On the basis of the discussion above, it may be useful to consider the distinctions between outside production of commercial services, as discussed in this study, and contracting for weapons systems, which has developed widely reported problems.[35] At its simplest, the services being considered in this study are inspection services or experience services that require only simple and inexpensive testing that can be carried out quickly and easily. That is, the commercial services are well understood, objective measures of performance can be developed and easily assessed, costs of changing producers are low, and many firms are equipped to supply the service. Major weapons systems are experience goods that may require long periods of expensive testing or long periods of use before the quality of the system is known.[36] Information on quality is very costly to obtain, there are few qualified producers, switching producers could be very costly, and performance criteria are extremely complex. In addition, the technology involved is in the experimental stage in which there is considerable inherent uncertainty about the quality that can be achieved with the technology, even in ideal circumstances. This means that the producer is likely to have much better information about the problems and opportunities for the system than is the buyer. All of this potentially makes quality assessment of weapons systems extremely difficult, but this is not to say that contracting for these systems is not cost effective. Rather, it indicates that outside production of complex weapons systems is almost certain to involve many more complex issues than contracting and other forms of competition for the commercial types of services considered in this study.[37]

In summary, the incentives created by market competition are the best available guarantors of cost minimization, but product characteristics may make it prohibitively expensive for buyers to obtain the information necessary to make the market function efficiently. Use of the market to obtain government-financed services is likely to be the most efficient when the services are well understood, objective measures of performance can be developed, costs of changing producers are relatively low, and several firms are capable of supplying the service.

This summary of optimal service characteristics for outside production of the government-financed service has been generally supported by the findings from collections of case studies and statistical studies covering several cities and services. Valente and Manchester (1984), who studied many individual cases in which cities had provided increased competition in producing government-financed services, concluded that total cost savings are most likely when the product is well defined enough to write a specific contract and when several potential private suppliers are already active in the producing similar services. Similarly, both Borcherding, Pommerehne, and Schneider (1982), and Bendick (1982) in their reviews of empirical studies concluded that

> the probability that privatization will be successfully implemented and will be preferable to government service delivery is strongly associated with certain prerequisites. Among these are: relatively narrow objectives, readily defined and easily measured; specifiable tasks and well-known production processes, monitorable at modest cost; a number of willing and able competing private sector suppliers; and a competent, honest government to enforce the rules of a fair market.

This summarization also closely follows the list of characteristics, found in the vertical integration literature[38] and in the total cost savings rates found in A-76 reviews,[39] favoring buying on the market rather than in-house production. The research on total cost savings from increased competition tabularized in Table 3.2 is also generally consistent with this conclusion. The newer studies, like the older ones, show substantial incremental total cost savings from increased competition, and much less stellar results when privatization is undertaken without competition or when competition is already in place.[40] Studies testing the effects of increased competition from intergovernmental competition and interagency competition also produce strong evidence of major cost savings.

REASONS FOR INCREASED TOTAL COSTS IN SOLE-SOURCE IN-HOUSE PRODUCTION OF GOVERNMENT-FINANCED SERVICES

As stated above, a primary rationale for producing government-financed services under more competitive conditions (e.g., outside production) is to reduce social costs. Three alternative rationales for expecting excessive costs, when these services are produced in-house by the government (cells I and II), are described below.

Attenuated Property Rights

Absent significant market failures, competition creates incentives for efficient production; this will be true whether the service is privately or publicly produced. Under competition, organizations that supply higher-quality and lower-price products are likely to attract more customers and be more profitable than those that supply lower-quality and higher-price products. In the limit, firms that fail to meet the challenges of competition will exit from the market and investors, managers, and other personnel associated with the firm may find this a costly process. In contrast, managers and workers in both private and government monopolies often face very limited competition for consumers' patronage, and, therefore, lack incentives to increase quality and decrease prices.[41] Further, particularly in public monopolies, managers and workers may share in little, if any, of the efficiency gains from superior performance and suffer few consequences from poor performance.[42] Without incentives to perform well, they cannot be expected to be as efficient as they might in more competitive circumstances.[43]

One prominent explanation for cost inefficiency in in-house government production is the "X-inefficiency" hypothesis.[44] This hypothesis posits that bureaucrats operating in a monopoly setting may pursue goals that unnecessarily increase costs.[45] In this model, excess costs stem from pursuit of the "easy life" in which difficult or controversial management decisions associated with efficient production are seldom made.[46]

Other economists have portrayed bureaus as a type of special interest group. In this view of the organizational environment, bureaus and taxpayers have divergent interests in minimizing costs, but citizens are relatively disorganized because the benefits of opposing excessive government expenditures are widely dispersed and the free-rider problem is severe.[47] This makes it difficult to induce taxpayers to incur the costs of effectively opposing excessive expenditures.[48] Income increases from excessive government expenditures, on the other hand, are concentrated among a relatively small number of bureau personnel who are therefore more easily organized.

The key implication of both theories is that efficiency in providing government-financed services is unlikely without competition in producing these services. In the X-inefficiency theory, the possibility of outside production makes the cost advantage of low-cost producers more obvious and relevant. This gives bureaus a greater incentive to minimize costs because low-cost bureaus have a higher probability of continuing to operate, whereas higher-cost ones are more likely to be displaced.[49] In the interest group theory, alternative suppliers of government services reduce the relative advantages of bureaus by forming a well-organized and well-informed countervailing interest group that often opposes the interests of budget-maximizing government bureaus or challenges coalitions between politicians and bureaus that exclude competition.[50]

Rules and Regulations Applied to
Commercial Government Services

Efficiency within government organizations that produce services that could be produced privately (i.e., government produced private services, cell II in Figure 1.1, and government produced commercial public services, part of cell I) may be impeded by application of rules and regulations designed to prevent politicalization or corruption of other parts of that government. In sections of the government that provide what many regard as inherently governmental services, such rules may be important. However, the application of these rules to all in-house production may lead to inefficiencies by needlessly raising operating costs, as explained below. Yet it may be difficult to operate parts of the government under antipoliticalization rules and other parts of the government under operating rules appropriate for private services.[51] Moving a service from in-house production, where such rules may have to apply, to outside production, where such rules are less necessary and less common, may improve efficiency.

Civil service rules (for example, the formalized procedures for hiring and firing) were, in part, initiated to insulate the bureaucracy from undue political influence. Although this may be an important aspect in operating inherently governmental activities where important discretionary decisions might easily be influenced contrary to the public interest, insulation of this type seems much less vital where standardized operations predominate. Reducing management's ability to hire and fire in such circumstances may impose costs by reducing workers' incentives to work hard and follow necessary routines, without providing any commensurate benefits.

Additional Unofficial Goals Adopted When Government Produces Services

Cost efficiency within government agencies may also be decreased because the agency pursues goals other than delivering the best service for the lowest cost.[52] Other goals adopted by the agency may conflict with the quality and cost goals that private firms would be expected to pursue exclusively. Pursuit of these other goals may require higher costs, but because they never appear in budget figures, public attention is not focused on these costs.[53] At least in some cases, it seems likely that explicit consideration of spending public money for these unannounced purposes would lead to rejection of these expenditures, but because they remain hidden within a monopoly agency's budget, the expenditure persists in the form of higher costs in agencies. If the agency faced competition, competitors without the need to meet unofficial goals with their hidden costs, could bid lower and would win the competition unless the agency shed the extraneous goal or obtained explicit funding to cover it.[54]

An example of this type of unrecognized cost occurred when costs of complying with dairy antisubstitution laws were imposed on state agencies at the time that margarine was introduced as a lower-price substitute for butter. When margarine started winning consumer acceptance on grocery store shelves, several states with high levels of dairy production outlawed the use of margarine in prison food service operations.[55] The apparent purpose of this restriction was to increase demand for milk products. Although this restriction increased the price of feeding prisoners (or reduced the quality or quantity of the other food provided), the cost of the restriction was never made explicit in the budgets for prisons. If competition for providing prison food services had been active during the period of these laws, state prison agencies with the margarine restriction would have been at a cost disadvantage in competing with firms or other jurisdictions without the margarine restrictions. Such competition could have resulted in removing these restrictions or at least making their costs explicit.

MEANS OF PROVIDING COMPETITION IN PRODUCTION OF GOVERNMENT-FINANCED SERVICES

For government-produced commercial services, three forms of increasing competition will be distinguished: The first of these is competition between private suppliers and government agencies. This is termed competitive privatization, and broad application of competitive privatization is a relatively recent addition to the array of sources of competition available to governments. Much of the evidence of resource savings from increased competition in government-financed services concerns competitive privatization. The two other forms of increasing competition are (1) introducing competition between or among political jurisdictions (e.g., two cities) and (2) introducing competition between agencies within a jurisdiction.

Competitive Privatization

At its simplest, privatization is the decision of a jurisdiction to curtail producing a service in-house in favor of production by an outside organization, usually a private one.[56] The focus here is on the form of privatization in which production is shifted to another organization (e.g., a private firm) through a competitive selection and contracting process, while the original jurisdiction finances production and retains some responsibility for the "quality" of the results.[57] This will be termed competitive privatization. Although not strictly privatization, a similar approach is to invite competition from both public and private suppliers and contract with the low bidder or bidders regardless of their form of ownership. Open competition between public and private suppliers will also be included under competitive privatization in this study.

Competitive privatization usually takes place through the process of opening a government service for bids by other organizations outside (or inside) the government that have produced a similar service in another context. A government undertaking competitive privatization of a service (1) prepares specifications of the service so that bidders can make their cost estimates, (2) establishes procedures for monitoring performance, and (3) solicits bids from qualified providers. Many governments simultaneously sponsor a management review of the agency currently providing the service. The goal of the review is to allow the agency to prepare its own bid to retain production of the service in-house. In management reviews, bids from private contractors provide two vital services. First, they are a yardstick against which to measure in-house costs. Without such a yardstick, there is no way to gauge the "true" costs of in-house production. Second, the presence of an actual competitor gives increased incentives for management and workers to cooperate in assessing potential cost savings. Top-down management reviews, in which evaluators have no real choices, or have only the choice of switching managers, may not elicit the kind of careful scrutiny that reduces costs to the fullest extent. Absent the competitive privatization reviews, these internal reorganizations have not and probably would not take place. Accordingly, the consideration of competitive privatization may produce efficiency gains even if government continues producing the service.

Privatization may be undertaken for any of a wide range of purposes from increasing worker incentives and reducing costs, to increasing community involvement in service decisions, to increasing short-run government revenues.[58] The latter two may or may not involve a strong element of competition. Although reasons for privatization span a wide range, the emphasis in this study is on the first reason mentioned for privatization: reducing the real costs of providing government financed services.

Intergovernmental Competition

An alternative check on inefficiencies in public production could be competition between jurisdictions.[59] If competition between jurisdictions were vigorous, it could be argued that governments would be forced by this form of competition to select the most efficient form and structure for supplying services or risk loosing their tax base as both individuals and industries move to more efficiently managed jurisdictions.

The idea that governments may compete with each other is termed the Tiebout hypothesis.[60] Tiebout posited that beneficial innovations in government services will spread because of competition between jurisdictions.[61] Jurisdictions providing lower cost services are more attractive to prospective residents because they can offer more or better services and lower taxes. Attracting new residents and commercial investment allows the jurisdiction to reduce average fixed costs by spreading them over a larger number of residents. Economic growth also is often associated with gains for incumbent residents as the value of extant properties increases with the increase in demand.

A related hypothesis has been put forward by Brennan and Buchanan (1980).[62] They hypothesize that areas with many local governments will have a smaller and more efficient public sector because competition between jurisdictions constrains the size of government. In addition, where governmental units are small, organizing the electorate within a jurisdiction to constrain the size and enhance the efficiency of government may be less difficult.

Intergovernmental competition, as hypothesized by Tiebout (1956) and Brennan and Buchanan (1980), is conceptually similar to ordinary competition between firms. The expected benefits of intergovernmental competition are similar to those expected from interfirm competition including lower costs, better quality, and increases in innovation. The primary difference is that governments do not directly have a profit incentive to serve consumers' interests. However, increased compensation, job security, or prestige, financed by economic growth, may be reasonable substitutes for the profit motive.

In many or most cases, direct competition between jurisdictions can be expected to operate only slowly to introduce service supply innovations. Several factors, such as moving costs, restrictions on moving elsewhere,[63] lack of information about conditions in other jurisdictions, family ties, and political opposition from those who benefit from excessive costs (per unit of output),[64] all may serve to mitigate the effects of competition between jurisdictions. The conditions favorable to competition between jurisdictions are weakest at the national level where the transaction costs of moving to another country are likely to be high and where restrictions on entry into another jurisdiction are common.[65] Although it is conceivable that policies to facilitate intergovernmental competition could be implemented, there is a natural reluctance on the part of any individual jurisdiction to make itself more vulnerable to competitive forces, and higher levels of government may be reluctant to increase this form of competition because constituent jurisdictions might be expected to oppose it.[66]

Direct effects are not the only mechanism through which intergovernmental competition can be felt. Intergovernmental competition may also take place indirectly as officials compare their jurisdictions' costs to those of other jurisdictions. Yardstick competition of this type does not depend on actual competition between jurisdictions, rather it is an information source that citizens and officials can use to identify innovative programs and financial arrangements that save taxpayers' money. Leagues of professional city managers, such as the International City Management Association (ICMA), work to increase the flow of such information as one of the goals of the profession.[67] Incentives to utilize comparative information to increase efficiency are strongest when budget constraints force officials to search for ways to reduce expenditures while maintaining services. Professional norms, political competition within a jurisdiction, and prestige may also be incentives for intergovernmental competition.

Although the effectiveness of direct intergovernmental competition may be limited, jurisdictions can provide additional long-term competitive discipline by borrowing for capital projects in private capital markets. The competitive discipline comes from the controls and incentives that lenders impose on borrowers.[68] All these controls and incentives are designed to ensure that the lender is repaid both interest and principal on the loan.

The fullest capital market discipline occurs in the context of loans that are guaranteed only by the proceeds from operating a particular service or facility. In revenue loans of this type, jurisdictions compete with each other for access to capital on the basis of their ability to meet revenue projections. A reputation for reasonable plans and efficient operation of similar facilities are directly rewarded by lower interest rates since the perceived risk to lenders is lower. Revenue loans place direct responsibility for efficiency in the hands of the management and failure to operate efficiently has direct and important negative effects on both future borrowing rates of the government involved and on the career prospects of the managers. Capital markets are generally well regarded as efficient allocators of capital and so governments that borrow in this fashion face considerable fiscal discipline compared to governments that finance through tax revenues or borrowing on their ability to tax (general obligation bonds). Empirical evidence of the cost-reducing effects of revenue bonds is dramatic.[69]

Interagency Competition

Most jurisdictions assign the task of providing a particular service to one (and only one) bureau. Under some relatively narrow circumstances this may be economically efficient,[70] however, in many other circumstances monopoly production may not enhance efficiency. An attractive alternative may be to allow two or more agencies to produce the service and to compete against each other in the manner of private firms.

Even if only one agency currently produces the service, the ability to switch a service between bureaus can establish incentives for managers and workers to increase quality and to control costs. This is probably most effective when shifting a service to another agency brings extrinsic rewards of increased pay and greater job security to managers and workers in that agency, but intrinsic rewards of prestige and elan may also be significant inducements for an agency to compete to gain additional services from other agencies.

To date, there has been relatively little research done on the possibilities of cost savings through internal competition between bureaus within a single jurisdiction, in part, because it is an infrequently used strategy. Most commonly, switches in assignments appear to be a last resort when a crisis of confidence occurs.[71] In a few instances, competition between agencies has been institutionalized, but it is unclear in most of these cases whether the competition was established to reduce cost and improve quality, or to institutionalize different points of view or avenues of control in carrying out particular functions.[72] Regardless of the reasons for competition, incentives for improvements in performance are greater when competition is present.[73]

There is one type of competition between government agencies that has been studied, competition between similar agencies at different levels of government. Under the Lakewood Plan, as this sort of competitive arrangement is called, local jurisdictions have the choice of contracting for a service with the county (or a neighboring local government) or providing it in-house.[74] Officials can compare the costs of in-house production and purchasing the service from the county. This gives the county agencies an incentive to minimize their costs to attract "business" (with attendant increased job security, promotion possibilities, and prestige) and it sets a cost standard against which officials can compare their in-house production costs. When in-house production offers the possibility of additional services, the incremental cost of such services can be ascertained by referring to the county rate. In summary the Lakewood arrangement provides information to officials on costs and create incentives for individual government agencies to minimize costs and improve quality of the services.

Summary

Three forms of competition are available to increase incentives for efficiency in government financed services. Two involve actual or potential displacement of in-house production by outside production. In the case of competitive privatization, private firms are the alternative suppliers. In the case of interagency competition, the alternative supplier is another government agency in the same or another jurisdiction. The third source of competition is intergovernmental competition. Here, competition acts indirectly through access to capital or efforts to attract investment and new residents.

All three forms of competition have demonstrable effects that will be discussed more fully in the remaining chapters, however, intergovernmental and interagency competition have found limited application or involve considerable lags. In contrast, competitive privatization has found wide application and considerable evidence about its effects is now available. Consequently, although intergovernmental and interagency evidence will be included where available, the bulk of the discussion will necessarily relate to competitive privatization and the effects of potential competitive privatization.

CONCLUSION

Governments finance a wide variety of services and historically most of these services have been produced in-house. For some services, in-house production is appropriate because these services are inherently governmental, that is, they involve extensive discretion and value judgments tied closely to powers that are reserved for the government. For many other services, termed commercial services, outside production is a possibility. Outside production is easiest when (1) there are multiple potential suppliers, (2) costs of switching from one producer to another are low, (3) information about the production process and supplier performance is relatively inexpensive to obtain, and (4) the service being provided can be clearly defined. Inability to institute incentives and controls in in-house government production also increases the probability that increased competition would increase efficiency.

Interest in outside production arises because there are several reasons to believe that in-house production is inefficient. Costs might be expected to rise above the competitive norm because in-house production may involve attenuation of incentives to minimize costs, application of costly rules protecting the integrity of inherent governmental services but encompassing all government services, and additional unofficial goals that increase costs. Increasing competition in producing government financed services can limit these cost increasing effects and should save valuable resources.

Although the theoretical case for increasing competition in in-house government financed commercial services is strong, much of the current interest can be traced to empirical evidence that increased competition promotes efficiency. Efforts to quantify the cost effects of increased competition on more than a case study basis have expanded greatly over the past decade. Major studies conducted by the federal government have included: the *Grace Commission Report*;[75] a Housing and Urban Development Department (HUD) report *Delivering Municipal Services Efficiently* (Stevens, 1984); studies from the Government Accounting Office and the Congressional Budget Office; and, most recently, *Privatization: Toward More Effective Government*, by the President's Commission on Privatization. Academic researchers and private public interest groups have also made numerous efforts to quantify some of the cost effects of increased competition.[76]

Each of the previous reports has focused on a particular aspect or portion of competitivization.[77] The objective of this study is to pull these disparate sources together to produce more generalized estimates of the cost effects of increasing competition in government-financed services produced in-house. This involves assembling the available estimates, revising them where appropriate, projecting the cost savings to a wider base where necessary, and summarizing the projections. The next two chapters examine federal and state/local overall cost savings estimates. Chapter 4 reviews studies separating real resource savings from distributional effects of increased competition. Chapter 5 draws the federal and state/local estimates from chapters 2, 3, and 4 together. Chapter 5 also provides summary remarks and discusses implications of the study for domestic and international efforts to improve economic efficiency and consumer welfare by increasing competition in government-financed services.

NOTES

1. Among social reformers and social scientists other than economists, interest in increasing government efficiency has a long history. The reformed government movement in the late nineteenth century was an early effort to improve government efficiency. It held that inefficiency could be reduced by removing patronage and favoritism from administration. At the same time, Weber and other sociologists were developing theories of organizations driven by an interest in improving government efficiency. The reformed government movement was followed by the progressive movement in the early twentieth century and by the accompanying academic study of "scientific management." Scientific management, a blend of social psychology and physiology, held that detailed evaluation and control of individual tasks could increase efficiency in government and in private enterprise (President's Commission on Privatization, 1988, chapter 11). Despite the long record of concern for government efficiency, it is only recently that increasing competition has become perceived as a vehicle for accomplishing this end. For example, virtually no references to potential cost savings through increased competition in providing government services appear in widely used public administration texts and commentaries prior to the mid-1970s. For example, see Sharkansky (1975) and Simon, Smithburg, and Thompson (1950).

2. Blankart (1987).

3. The term services, in this context, could apply to both goods and services, but the focus of this report is on services.

4. Musgrave and Musgrave (1976, chapter 3). Economists have suggested that public services (goods) can be provided privately in many circumstances through franchise arrangements with private firms. In this scenario, government no longer finances the service, it does however, monitor compliance with the franchise agreement. See Demsetz (1968) for a modern elaboration of this theory, originally propounded by Edwin Chadwick, a Victorian social reformer. The present study focuses on services that continue to be financed by government.

Although public services are conceptually distinct from private services, categorizing a specific service as one or the other can be difficult because many services appear to have both public and private service aspects.

5. This is termed the problem of revealed preferences for public goods.

6. In an assessment of the efficiency of government providing a service, costs of raising government revenues should be considered. There are a wide variety of such costs. See Seldon (1982, p. 160).

7. If consumers in a jurisdiction do not have homogeneous valuations of the public good, some consumers may be forced to contribute more toward the public goods than these goods are worth to them. This would reduce efficiency. The efficiency effects of government financing of public services should be positively related to the homogeneity of consumer valuations within the jurisdiction.

The efficiency effects of government financing may also be lessened if choices are limited to a few dissimilar bundles of services and taxes. See the section on attenuated property rights for additional discussion.

8. For a more extensive discussion of the choice between in-house and outside production, see the section on vertical integration.

9. Competition from another government's agency might not be considered inappropriate for some inherently governmental services. The other government's agency would be supervised and monitored by its own citizens in ways that would protect the interests of all the people it serves. For example, police contracted from one jurisdiction to perform police duties for another jurisdiction might be expected to respect the rights of citizens from both jurisdiction equally because it is expected that the same rules of conduct will be applied to all of the contracting police department's operations.

10. Government operated services that are financed through user fees, rather than through government tax revenues, are not directly covered by Figure 1.1. Since user fees are a form of market rationing, the successful utilization of user fees to finance a service implies that the service is not a pure public service. If a service is a pure public service, few would willingly pay a user fee. Hence publicly produced services financed by user fees are likely to be at least partially private services and are best considered as part of cell II. Publicly produced services financed by user fees are also reasonable

11. A dramatic change in technology might also shift a service from one cell to another. For example, a change in technology might make it economically feasible to exclude those who do not pay. This would make the good or service more private and less public and move the service toward cell II from cell I.

12. In this case, the economy is characterized by cells I and II in Figure 1.1.

13. Peters (1986) discussing La Mirada, California. In this case, the production of government financed public and private services falls into cells III and IV.

14. In particular, the estimates of cost savings in chapters 2 and 3 are based on studies of total cost savings.

15. Coincidentally, by allowing additional types of suppliers to compete, these methods of increasing competition in cells I and II may have effects on competition in cells III and IV.

16. Market failure rationales for in-house production of services include the following: (1) independence from private (economic) interests (e.g., court systems and police); (2) direct control by the government (army, embassies, law enforcement); (3) security in supply (energy, mail, railway, and other public utilities like gas, electricity, and water); (4) quality standards and orientation toward socially meritorious goals (television, theaters, schools, universities); (5) preventing misuse of monopoly or oligopoly power and destructive competition (insurance and banking sectors); (6) realization of the social benefits of risky private investments and innovations (basic scientific research, exploration of space); (7) pursuit of social distributional goals (all regions have to be equally supplied with traffic control, postal services, etc., price discrimination between poor and rich); (8) protection of jobs due to structural changes (coal and steel industry) and for social reasons (employment of disabled persons). Other rationales for in-house production of commercial services may include: tradition, political support, legal restrictions imposed by higher levels of government, switching costs, insufficient alternative suppliers, and other sources of competitive incentives.

Efficiency rationales for government production are discussed in the section on vertical integration.

17. See Savas (1990) for description of various approaches to shedding services.

18. Although reducing wage premiums and other economic rents is not the primary focus of this study, some governments facing budget restraints may be interested in lower expenditure levels whether the savings come from real resource savings or from reduced wage premiums with uncertain real resource implications.

19. Vertical integration involves ownership of one stage in the production of a product by an organization involved in another stage of production for the same product. For example, if an electrical utility determines to purchase a coal mine to fuel its generating facilities, the utility is vertically integrating. For a general treatment of vertical integration, see Blair and Kaserman (1983).

20. Major contributions to this literature include Coase (1937), Williamson (1975, 1979), Goldberg (1976), Alchian and Demsetz (1972), Arrow (1974), and Nelson and Winter (1973). Early concern about transaction costs in the context of clashes between owners' and managers' interests appeared in Berle and Means (1932).

21. The sources of this problem include, for example, technological interdependency, relationship specific investments, cost of making contracts (cost of revealing true risks), unenforceability of contracts, high information costs, economies in gathering information to operate and monitor compliance with the contract, market power, externalities, uncertainty, bilateral monopoly, efficiencies of vertical integration in coordinating responses to rapid changes in demand or supply conditions, and moral hazard. (Moral hazard occurs when opportunities arise for a firm or individual to gain by taking advantage of contract terms designed to accommodate uncertainty about future conditions. For example, if a contract calls for a cost plus payment in order to accommodate uncertainty about inflation, the contractee may have less incentive to minimize costs than if the contract did not allow such adjustments. See Williamson [1975, pp. 96-98] for an example of such behavior in manufacturing.) Where these types of conditions dominate, it may be more efficient to integrate production within a single organization.

22. Greer (1984, pp. 382-85).

23. U.S. automobile manufacturers appear to be shifting away from vertical integration in an effort to match the cost advantages apparently obtained by Japanese automobile manufacturers using "just in time" delivery from independent suppliers. See Kwoka (1989, pp. 67-72).

24. See, for example, Walker and Weber (1984, pp. 373-91). The interorganizational dependence perspective in organizational theory also is concerned with vertical integration. This perspective is described by Aiken and Hage and Yuchtman and Seashore, in Maurer (1971).

25. See Adams (1977, p. 99) and Weiss (1961, pp. 329-50).

26. Klein, Crawford, and Alchian (1978). More recently, see Coase (1988a, 1988b).

27. The economic analysis of corruption emphasizes the potential significance of overpayments as a device to create incentives for honesty. Since the value of the stream of overpayments is lost if corrupt practices are detected, participating in corrupt practices carries additional risk. Neugebauer (1978). Interestingly, consumer economics suggests that a price premium on high-quality branded products acts in a similar way by giving producers an incentive not to lower quality. See, for example, Shapiro (1983).

28. Three important differences between private and public vertical integration conditions should be noted before proceeding. First, public officials probably have less flexibility in creating incentives for public agency managers to reduce costs than do private boards of directors supervising private managers. Lack of flexibility in creating internal incentives should result in greater advantages to producing outside. Second, public officials often have less readily identifiable standards for

measuring success. Lack of readily identifiable criteria makes it more difficult to use arms-length market (contract) relations as a substitute for internal production. Third, public officials have the authority to tax. The power to tax increases the ability of public decision makers to avoid effective competition since revenues are not based on voluntary purchases, but this does not necessarily present an obstacle to relying on outside production of government financed services.

29. Williamson (1975, summarized at p. 104).

30. This section is largely derived from Blankart (1987).

A popularized version of this categorization scheme is the distinction between "hard" (inspection and experience) and "soft" (credence) government services. See Valente and Manchester (1984, chapter 1, especially, p. 13).

31. Even in this case, it might be possible to contract with individual jurists or arbitrators who have the requisite education and agree to abide by specified procedures. The Federal Trade Commission has utilized arbitrators to handle consumer complaints about warranty coverage in a number of cases. See U.S. Federal Trade Commission (1980) and Palfrey and Romer (1986) for discussion.

32. Self-manufacture by consumers might be considered just the most extreme form of vertical integration.

33. The best known work in this area is Klein and Leffler (1981). For a review of consumer protection literature generally, see Ippolito (1986). Experimental findings in consumer economics are discussed in Lynch, Miller, Plott, and Porter (1986).

34. The presence of learning and reputation effects suggests that government may benefit from contractual terms for outside production that are short, unless sunk costs or other switching costs are significant.

35. Pound and Carrington (1988).

36. It also could be that major weapons systems involve substantial uncertainty about quality both for the supplier and the government, even after completion. Complex contracting terms that provide for risk sharing may be an option in such cases.

37. Often long-term, multiproject contracts and various cost sharing arrangements, as well as competition, are adopted in an effort to maintain efficiency incentives in procuring such complex systems.

38. Vertical integration was reviewed at the beginning of this section.

39. The federal government's A-76 program is reviewed in chapter 2.

40. See particularly, Savas (1981).

41. Improvements in quality and lower prices are elements of allocative efficiency, that is, the optimal choice of outputs given society's limited resources, assuming all production occurs at minimum costs.

42. Minimizing costs for any given level of output is termed production efficiency. Production efficiency is assumed in discussions of allocative efficiency.

43. See Alchian (1965); Simon, Smithburg, and Thompson (1950, Chapter 3); Tullock (1965); Lindsay (1976); Downs (1967, Chapter 8); and Thompson (1969). Also see Pommerehne and Schneider (1985). See Appendix A for an explanation of the social costs and income transfers involved.

44. The X-inefficiency hypothesis applies to both private and public bureaucracies. In both cases, X-inefficiency is related to agency problems. An agency problem arises when the private interests of decisions makers differ from those of owners. In private firms the managers may have different incentives than stock holders. In public organizations, policy makers and bureau managers may have different incentives than citizens generally. In general one might expect the problems of organizing investor interests to be somewhat easier than organizing the broader general citizenship interest, and therefore the degree of X-inefficiency to be less in a private monopoly than in a government monopoly.

An alternative explanation for higher than necessary costs in government production was developed by Niskanen (1971).

45. See Migue and Belanger (1974) and Brenton and Wintrobe (1975). Also see Leibenstein (1976) for a more general exposition of slack in organizations.

Although most models of managerial self-interest suggest that increased efficiency will accompany increased competition, for example, Hart (1983), some do not. See, for example, Scharfstein (1988). Scharfstein assumes a different set of managerial incentives. He assumes that managers will obtain more insulation of their salaries (insurance of salary levels) when the environment is more competitive (risky). The increase in insulation may reduce efficiency incentives by more than competition enhances efficiency incentives.

46. See Appendix A for a discussion of social welfare losses from this type of digression from the competitive ideal.

DeVaney (1976) has suggested an alternative interpretation of x-inefficiency and other types of excess capacity in the context

47. Free riding occurs when it is difficult to exclude consumers from obtaining a good or service even if they have not paid for it. In this context, citizens who contribute nothing to organizing efforts to increase government efficiency gain just as much as those who do not contribute.

48. Olson (1965). Also see Lentz (1981) and Courant, Gramlich, and Rubenfield (1980).

Some empirical work supports the hypothesis that tighter citizen control is associated with reduced costs. Pommerehne and Schneider (1983) found that municipalities with strong citizen control averaged 15% to 30% lower costs, primarily because such control restrained wage increases. Also see Pommerehne and Frey (1978).

Also see the section on competitive privatization in this chapter that describes forms of intergovernmental competition.

49. In Niskanen's theory, outside production can establish limits on the size of the government sector by providing elected officials with increased information on minimum costs. When officials are aware of their options, failure to present a budget that minimizes costs will increase the probability that the bureaucracy will be displaced by outside producers. See Niskanen (1971,1975).

50. For a model of privatization including both elements, see Bos (1987).

51. Reforming internal government operating rules to create incentives for government managers to operate as efficiently as possible is an area of reform that could be studied more thoroughly. Frug (1987) strongly makes this case and similar ideas are expressed in American Federation of State, County, and Municipal Employees (AFSCME) (1983, pp. 99-100).

52. Millward (1982) and Frug (1987). Perhaps the most significant argument of this type is that costs are higher in government because laws embodying additional values and goals are better enforced in government operations. In this view, privatization reduces expenditures because it broadens the application of illegal, but lower-cost, practices. See Asher's and Popkin's (1984) critique of Perloff and Wachter (1984), for example. Asher and Popkin attribute higher U.S. Postal Service labor costs to less race and sex discrimination in the U.S. Postal Service than in private firms. For additional discussion, see chapter 4.

53. When program costs are made explicit, the budget is said to be transparent.

54. Although contractors may be required to satisfy additional unofficial goals, the contract has to make these transparent because the for-profit contractor has an incentive to avoid such costs (because extra costs decrease profits) if the contract does not make this aspect of performance explicit.

55. Riepma (1970).

56. Competitive privatization finds a parallel in the decisions of firms to buy from outside suppliers or contract out aspects of their production processes. An important incentive in both public and private decisions of this type is the relative efficiency of in-house or outside production. See the previous discussion of vertical integration.

57. See Demsetz (1968). Our focus limits consideration of user fees, voucher systems (such as the G.I. Bill that financed college education for many veterans after World War II), and tax rebate systems. See Bendick

(1982) for a review of voucher experiments suggesting that voucher systems have shown mixed results. See the President's Commission on Privatization (1988) for a more favorable treatment. Voucher systems assume that consumers are able to make informed decisions and should be allowed and encouraged to do so. Voucher programs generally work poorly in programs that are designed to control consumers' consumption patterns. On rebate systems, see Walberg, Bakalis, Bast, and Baer (1988). On user fees, see Gillette and Hopkins (1987). Financing projects through user fees instead of general revenues introduces the concept of pricing into public services. Such prices may cause consumers to recognize the costs of government-produced goods and services that they consume. In some cases, public demand for a service may be sensitive to price. If so, the lack of an effective rationing mechanism may lead government to overproduce the good. A second use of user fees is to signal the government producer about the level of demand, given these costs. User fees can also alert private producers about opportunities to compete in providing a service. Without accurate price signals from user fees, private producers are unlikely to consider entry, and the advantages of lower-cost production techniques that they might employ will not be realized. For example, if government subsidizes production of a certain quantity of a particular service, otherwise financed by user fees, private competitors will be at a competitive disadvantage in serving the subsidized part of the market. If so, private producers may have to operate at an inefficient scale.

58. A 1982 survey by the International City Management Association, reported in Valentine and Manchester (1984), provides the best information about which local government services are most commonly provided by private organizations. See Table 3.4 and the section in chapter 3 on the extent of in-house commercial services for more discussion. Appendix D reviews more recent research findings on shifts in the patterns of privatization of municipal services.

59. In an environment in which budget constraints become appreciably more binding, as they arguably did in the late 1970s and early 1980s, political leaders may be forced to actively search for cost savings even if jurisdictions do not compete.

60. Tiebout (1956).

61. If a jurisdiction builds its infrastructure with substantial fixed costs to accommodate a given number of people and subsequently loses population because it provides these services inefficiently, the *fixed* costs will have to be spread among fewer tax payers. Taxes will have to be raised and the remaining residents will be worse off. A vicious cycle may develop in which remaining residents become progressively worse off.

62. Empirical tests of this hypothesis recently have been completed. This work suggests that having many small governments in an area does have some constraining effect in general purpose governments, but that economies of scale confound the effect in the case of single service governments. See Zax (1989), Forbes and Zampelli (1989), and Oates (1985, 1989). Some empirical work on interjurisdictional competition has also focused on difference between jurisdictions in the degree of citizen control. See, for example, Wagner and Weber (1975) for discussion and empirical support for the view that competition between governments and increased monitoring of in-house production can reduce costs.

63. Examples for businesses include pollution permits and zoning regulations. For individuals, examples include citizenship requirements and occupational licensing restrictions.

64. This factor is the subject of the extensive literature on public choice. See, for example, Mueller (1979).

65. Transactions costs include language and cultural barriers. Many countries restrict the number of immigrants who might compete for jobs with current citizens of the country.

66. Indeed, higher levels of government sometimes enact legislation that expressly inhibits interjurisdictional competition. The most prominent example is the tax exemption extended for payments of local and state taxes. By absorbing some of the cost to consumers of local taxes, the federal income tax rules hinder states and localities from competing on the basis of tax rates.

67. The city management profession arose in response to perceived corruption and inefficiency in government during the scientific management and progressive periods during the first quarter of the century. One of the selling points of the city management profession is more efficient management (President's Commission on Privatization, 1988, chapter 11).

68. Competition in the capital market is seen as major disciplinary force in markets generally. Williamson (1975, chapters 5, 6, 7, and 9).

69. See *Canada, Auditor General of, Report of 1985* (1985). Results of this study are reviewed in chapter 3. For a general treatment of credit ratings and government borrowing, see Peterson (1977).

Interest in access to the capital market may also impose more general fiscal discipline. Fiscal crises in several large U.S. cities partially can be explained by concern about retaining access to capital markets (Peterson, 1977).

70. Economic efficiency may be improved in a few narrow instances by monopoly. In the case of a single good or service industry, if economies of scale exist over much of, but not the entire output range, cost subadditivity may exist, in which case entry would increase total costs of production. (An "economy of scale" exists when the per item cost of

providing a good or service decreases as the quantity of production of that good or service increases.) If so, some limits on entry might reduce costs. See Baumol, Panzar, and Willig (1982, pp. 192-97), and Tirole (1988, pp. 309-10). Another rationale for legal protection of monopoly exists if demand is insufficient to cover long-run total costs absent price discrimination, and this price discrimination would be defeated by arbitrage unless legal restrictions on entry preserve the price discrimination.

No protection against entry is necessary if a single good industry has economies of scale over the whole relevant range of production, because the incumbent monopolist will be able to offer lower prices than any other prospective producers as long as it minimizes costs.

In the case of a multiproduct monopolist, a protected multiproduct monopoly may be justified by efficiency concerns if entry is otherwise completely unimpeded (the market is naturally contestable), economies of scale are relatively large, economies of scope are relatively small, and the different services produced by the monopoly are close substitutes in demand for each other. (An "economy of scope" exists when the cost of providing a set of goods or services is lower when they are produced together than when they are produced separately. A market is said to be contestable if there are no sunk, nonrecoverable costs associated with supplying the market or entrants can enter and reap monopoly profits before the incumbent firm(s) can cut prices.) Under these circumstances, a monopolist in both markets might not be able to successfully compete against an entrant that specializes in a subset of services unless the monopolist abandons one or more of the services that the monopolist initially provided. For an overview of this topic, see Baumol, Panzar, and Willig (1982), and Baumol, Panzar, and Willig (1986, pp. 339-70), and the references contained therein.

71. For example, the mayor of Washington, D.C. recently reassigned the management responsibility for the ambulance service from the fire department to the office of the city administrator after several life threatening lapses in quality in the city's ambulance service and difficulties in recruiting and training paramedics (Sherwood and Sanchez, 1988).

72. Perhaps the example that comes closest is President Roosevelt's purposeful institutionalization of multiple channels of information gathering. See Neustadt (1960, pp. 157-61). Other examples include the cojurisdiction over antitrust of the Federal Trade Commission and the Justice Department, overlapping intelligence gathering activities at the Central Intelligence Agency and National Security Agency, and maintenance of separate navy, army, and air force military commands.

73. In the case of government agencies, performance is the output of services that are valued by government decision makers who determine the level of resources available to the agencies. These performance

measures may or may not correspond to the value of these services to consumers.

74. Gordon (1984, pp. 115-19). Results of this research are reviewed in chapter 3.

75. *The President's Private Sector Survey on Cost Control* (1983).

76. See Table 3.6 in chapter 3.

77. Disagreements in defining competitivization and privatization have complicated the process of understanding the effects of both processes. See, for example, Clarkson (1989).

2

Federal Government
Potential Cost Savings

INTRODUCTION

The federal government, in addition to providing income transfers and paying interest on its debt, purchased $366 billion of goods and services in fiscal 1986. Of this, $143 billion, or about 40%, was compensation for government employees, half each for civilian and military personnel. Of the remaining $223 billion, one-third went for military procurement. Thus civilian support services for the military and all costs of other federal government agencies, totaled approximately $218 billion.[1] These services, as described in chapter 1, can be divided between commercial functions and inherently governmental functions.

The federal government has for some time had a program, the A-76 program, designed to increase efficiency in producing government financed commercial services through increased competition. Despite the long history of this program, it has not been applied to most government-produced commercial services to date. However, it has been applied in enough instances to provide a basis for estimating the cost savings that might be possible if a program of increased competition were fully implemented.[2]

Making estimates of cost savings requires information on (1) the rate of cost savings and (2) the magnitude of expenditures for in-house commercial services where increased competition may result in cost savings. The potential total cost savings are calculated by multiplying the expected rate of cost savings by expenditures for commercial services that are produced by in-house monopolies. Providing such a calculation for federal government activities is the goal of this chapter.

COST-SAVINGS RATES

Background Information on the Primary Source of Information on Cost Savings: The A-76 Program

Since 1955, the federal government has had a general policy of utilizing outside production of commercial services where possible. Since 1966, the policy has been to utilize outside production whenever doing so saves money, while maintaining necessary service quality.[3] Current procedures governing external contracting decisions are detailed in the Office of Management and Budget's (OMB) Circular A-76.[4]   The OMB's basic position is that the government should not compete with private producers, especially when government production is relatively inefficient. Agencies are directed by Circular A-76 to increase competition by relying on the private sector for commercial services whenever it is cost effective to do so and responsibilities can be defined in enough detail to monitor the quality of service received. The first step in the A-76 process is to identify services that are performed by federal employees that could be performed by the private sector. Next, the agency must undertake a detailed study of each such service. In the study, the agency must describe minimum work requirements and performance standards that it uses or will use to assess the quality of service provided.[5]   The agency must then ascertain the lowest cost at which the government can produce the service in-house after management reorganization or other steps to increase efficiency.[6]   This constitutes the government's "bid" in the competition with outside producers. Finally, the agency then must compare the government bid with the cost of operating the service with a competitively selected contractor. The agency must convert to contract performance if the lowest feasible in-house production cost exceeds the best contract price offer by 10% or more (or if no in-house bid is made).[7] The 10% differential is used to account for increased monitoring costs and disruptions caused by switching to an outside supplier.

Cost savings under this program may come from a winning contract bid that is less than the agency's original cost of providing the service, or, if the agency retains internal production, from lower costs that follow reorganization of in-house production.

Other than the Department of Defense (DOD), which has considerable experience with the A-76 process, few agencies have conducted extensive A-76 studies or identified significant numbers of commercial activities to be reviewed until very recently, despite repeated prompting from OMB.[8] Much of the nondefense service contracting occurs in the high-technology operations of the Department of Energy (DOE) and the National Aeronautics and Space Administration (NASA). Other agencies that have recently become more active include the Departments of Commerce and Transportation and the General Services Administration.   The DOD's reviews primarily involved "blue-collar" occupations for many years, but have recently included more administrative positions. Prominent on the list of services contracted to outside firms are cleaning services, cafeteria operations, and vehicle maintenance services. Both defense and nondefense agencies have been slow to review "white-collar" operations, such as secretarial services and computer operations.

Rates of Cost Savings from the A-76 Program

The most recent analysis of rates of cost savings from the A-76 program appears in a 1987 U.S. Congressional Budget Office (CBO) report.[9]   The CBO reviewed 180 functions (covering approximately 14,000 full-time equivalent government positions) studied under A-76 at DOD in 1984 and 1985. Using DOD data (and its own adjustments for changed circumstances),[10] the CBO estimates that A-76 studies result in decisions to contractout covering about 65% of both the functions and positions reviewed. In the remaining 35%, production remains in-house, but management and organizational structure are revamped to make in-house production costs more competitive with outside production costs.[11]

Cost savings average over 35% of the prereview costs in the DOD functions that were contracted out after A-76 studies, according to the CBO's evaluation.[12]   In the functions reviewed that remained in-house, internal management improvements generated cost savings of at least 20% on average. The average rate of savings for all functions reviewed under A-76 is over 30%.

Table 2.1 shows unadjusted data concerning A-76 cost savings at DOD for the years 1984 through 1986. The rate of savings shown in Table 2.1 exceeds the CBO's figures because the CBO adjusted its estimates downward to reflect two recent changes that would have reduced in-house government costs relative to outside production costs, if the changes had been in place during the observation period. These changes are (1) the revised retirement system for federal employees[13] and (2) a continuing sequence of cost-of-living adjustments that are less than the rate of inflation.

The CBO also adjusted the actual contract specific savings downward to reflect short-term adjustment costs in switching from in-house to outside production. These costs include: rebidding contracts where necessary, paying separation costs to workers who could not be successfully reassigned within the government, adjusting contracts for errors in specifying the tasks that have to be performed, and disrupting services during the transition from in-house to contract production.

Finally, the CBO estimates contain an adjustment to account for cost increases in contracts that may not be attributable to general economy-wide changes in cost conditions.[14]

The rate of cost reduction estimates found in the CBO study are in the same range as those obtained in earlier studies. Previous studies have produced estimates of direct cost savings in federal government services ranging from 10% to 30%, not including savings from reconfiguration of internal production.[15] We will use both the 10% and 30% rates to bound our cost-savings estimates.

Inherent in the process of estimating cost-savings rates are a number of potential sources of error. These sources of error may result in over estimates or under estimates. Some suggest that actual total cost savings are likely to be higher and some suggest they are likely to be lower.

Table 2.1
Defense Department Cost Reductions from
Increased Competition through Contracting and
Internal Management Improvements

	1984	1985	1986
Average Savings from Contracting	41%	38%	38%
Average Savings from Internal Management Improvement	22%	20%	23%

SOURCE: Musell (1987).

NOTE: Average savings are expressed as a percent of in-house costs before contracting out or management improvements.

Cost-savings estimates assume that contracting out occurs at a slow enough pace that jobs could be privatized without layoffs or with rehiring by the contractor.

Potential sources of error include inapplicability of DOD results to other agencies, declining average savings rates as more functions are examined, and using short-run rather than long-run cost-savings rates.

Regarding applicability of DOD results, the A-76 reviews at DOD have primarily involved services commonly utilized in other agencies such as vehicle maintenance and cleaning services. Hence, there is little reason to believe that DOD's experience should be unique.

Concerning declining average savings rates, there is no evidence that savings rates experienced at DOD have declined over time. At least in the army, programs scheduled for A-76 studies have been selected largely at random from among those that have been determined to be commercial services potentially suitable for transferring to private production.[16]   Both of these pieces of evidence argue against the hypothesis that A-76 reviews to date have been "cream skimming," but the expectation of eventually diminishing returns is too widely reported in other economic situations to be dismissed entirely.

Concerning short-run rather than long-run cost savings, although there do not appear to be any longitudinal studies in the competitive privatization literature of costs for samples of services newly subject to increased competition, it might be conjectured that cost savings would increase over time as equipment, training, and management techniques adjust more fully to the new incentives to improve efficiency.   It is commonly observed in economics generally that long-run adjustments to changes in costs or incentives are more thoroughgoing than short-run adjustments, and consequently the long-term adjustments are larger. If so, short-run cost-savings estimates, such as those provided here, may understate the magnitude of ultimate efficiency gains.

Another important set of cautions in interpreting these rates of total cost-savings estimates involves the institutional constraints in achieving such savings rates. No one should be under the illusion that all it takes is someone to give the word, and like magic, reviews for hundreds of thousands of jobs could be completed, with annual savings of billions of dollars.[17]   It cannot happen that quickly or that dramatically. Several important aspects of due process and practical considerations slow and limit the efforts to increase competition. (1) The process of increasing competition can be time consuming. Initial screening to separate inherently governmental from commercial functions has to be carried out. Next, the reviews themselves have to be conducted and staffing to conduct the reviews has to be arranged. Finally, the bidding and contracting phases have to be conducted in an orderly manner. (2) Some of the cost savings from increased competition are not immediate, even under the best of circumstances, since they involve reductions in long-term government liabilities that will not be realized for several years. (3) If program evaluations are accelerated, a smaller proportion of former employees could be accommodated through other job openings in the government. If so, costs from layoffs could increase.

The factors mentioned above imply that the cost-savings estimates are likely to be subject to significant errors in both directions. The purpose of the estimates is not to provide precise estimates, but rather to provide information about the general magnitude of potential total cost savings over the long-run and the range of potential savings.

EXPENDITURES ON IN-HOUSE COMMERCIAL SERVICES

Estimates of potential total cost savings from increased competition require information on the magnitude of current in-house expenditures on commercial services. Rates of cost savings can then be applied against this base to estimate potential cost savings. The magnitude of current expenditures on commercial in-house services can be assessed either by adding up expenditures for *programs* that involve commercial services or by adding up expenditures for *positions* that provide commercial services that could be produced outside of government.[18] Both the program and occupation methods may be used to provide estimates of total expenditures for commercial functions, if they are carried out in detail.[19] However, the position-based estimates should be used cautiously as an upper bound, at least with respect to competitive privatization, because many of these positions closely support inherently governmental activities. For such positions, even though it might be possible to contract out with private parties, doing so might undermine the security and integrity of the inherently governmental functions. Hence, it seems unlikely that all the commercial positions could or should be open to competition from private suppliers. Competition and resulting cost savings from intra- and interagency sources, however, need not be precluded from consideration on this basis.

At the federal level, the best available data on the extent of commercial services is based on occupational data. No systematic program-by-program estimates are yet available. Occupational data is systematically collected by the Office of Personnel Management (OPM) and consequently the estimates of in-house commercial operations in this chapter are based on these data. The broadest and most recent review of such position estimates is the 1987 CBO study.[20]

Although the OPM occupation data are the best available data set, they should be used with caution because of the possibility of miscounting commercial service production positions. Only more detailed program reviews can settle the question of which positions are actually commercial enough in character to warrant consideration by outside production and to assure that the position is not so closely tied to inherently governmental functions that outside competition, at least, would be inadvisable.

Table 2.2 shows the commercial occupations compiled by the CBO and identifies those that the CBO considered appropriate for review because they have commercial counterparts in the private sector. Policymaking, law enforcement, and revenue-related positions were eliminated from consideration by the CBO, even where private services of the same kind are available. The functions served by these excluded positions may be inherently governmental and therefore may be noncommercial.

The CBO conducted its occupation-by-occupation review of executive agencies without regard to existing exemptions to A-76 or to the apparent reluctance of many agencies to examine white-collar positions. The CBO estimated that up to 1.4 million federal executive department civilian workers perform commercial duties.[21]

Transforming position estimates into expenditure estimates requires multiplying the number of positions (1.4 million) by average costs per position. The CBO data are again used for the estimates. The CBO found that average total costs for programs reviewed under A-76 were approximately $40,000 per "full-time-equivalent" (FTE) employee.[22] This figure includes, for example, retirement, supplies and equipment, wages, and overhead. Earlier studies employed estimates of in-house production average costs per FTE position, ranging from $20,000 to $57,500 per employee. Table 2.3 compares the average expenditure and rate of average cost saving criteria utilized in earlier studies to those of the CBO study.[23] Using the CBO data, the total expenditure on in-house production of commercial services is estimated to be $56 billion.

Table 2.2
Civilian Full-Time Positions in Commercial Occupations

Occupation	State	Treasury	Defense
Miscellaneous	13	49	19,832
Social Science	35	11	5,703
Personnel	12	141	1,860
Admin. Clerical	4,706	33,076	167,700
Biology	3	0	2,214
Accounting	95	2,325	26,613
Medical	131	49	21,328
Veterinary	0	0	18
Engineering	163	343	80,068
Legal	49	581	948
Information	118	168	10,237
Business	3	78	5,585
Physical	81	270	16,669
Library	124	52	3,503
Math	3	227	8,509
Equipment	23	121	14,819
Education	193	82	24,029
Supply	43	334	42,403
Transportation	23	122	8,605
All White Collar	5,818	38,029	460,643
All Blue Collar	180	3,634	325,436
All Positions	5,998	41,663	786,079

Table 2.2 (continued)

Occupation	Justice	Interior	Agriculture
Miscellaneous	230	4,711	132
Social Science	747	1,011	644
Personnel	54	99	103
Admin. Clerical	13,118	8,540	13,173
Biology	22	5,100	20,504
Accounting	850	939	2,037
Medical	705	41	121
Veterinary	0	8	2,589
Engineering	477	4,761	5,501
Legal	2,731	561	263
Information	562	1,092	589
Business	14	988	585
Physical	257	8,964	2,839
Library	321	217	221
Math	175	124	987
Equipment	286	307	123
Education	351	3,065	256
Supply	226	403	247
Transportation	94	60	167
All White Collar	21,220	40,991	51,081
All Blue Collar	2,481	9,635	3,749
All Positions	23,701	50,626	54,830

Table 2.2 (continued)

Occupation	Commerce	Labor	HHS
Miscellaneous	90	840	184
Social Science	140	645	1,474
Personnel	21	35	56
Admin. Clerical	6,491	3,347	23,826
Biology	349	0	2,973
Accounting	498	223	1,193
Medical	9	504	12,497
Veterinary	2	0	93
Engineering	1,492	283	484
Legal	73	262	3,168
Information	296	94	591
Business	19	5	29
Physical	6,616	146	2,276
Library	226	46	495
Math	2,173	393	917
Equipment	77	20	120
Education	18	177	156
Supply	105	65	364
Transportation	41	4	60
All White Collar	18,736	7,089	50,960
All Blue Collar	1,466	0	4,584
All Positions	20,202	7,089	55,544

Table 2.2 (continued)

Occupation	Transport.	Personnel	GSA
Miscellaneous	345	0	119
Social Science	296	22	106
Personnel	52	13	42
Admin. Clerical	5,564	1,452	4,340
Biology	15	0	0
Accounting	724	69	922
Medical	168	8	7
Veterinary	1	0	0
Engineering	9,515	0	752
Legal	527	65	139
Information	177	22	86
Business	258	4	1,566
Physical	208	0	26
Library	63	7	9
Math	270	40	43
Equipment	135	7	114
Education	289	26	34
Supply	33	27	744
Transportation	4,487	0	268
All White Collar	23,127	1,762	9,317
All Blue Collar	3,981	0	8,926
All Positions	27,108	1,762	18,243

Table 2.2 (continued)

Occupation	NASA	TVA	Veterans Ad.
Miscellaneous	67	1,068	1,071
Social Science	90	962	5,984
Personnel	11	0	77
Admin. Clerical	2,490	2,752	25,094
Biology	54	143	1,697
Accounting	351	254	2,893
Medical	50	125	103,488
Veterinary	0	0	7
Engineering	8,584	4,794	1,573
Legal	77	67	790
Information	157	79	560
Business	22	12	395
Physical	1,195	645	608
Library	45	41	532
Math	551	35	171
Equipment	131	534	195
Education	13	35	517
Supply	62	0	2,215
Transportation	85	45	322
All White Collar	14,035	11,591	148,189
All Blue Collar	1,276	13,539	34,364
All Positions	15,311	25,130	182,553

Table 2.2 (continued)

Occupation	Subtotal	Other Agency	Total
Miscellaneous	28,751	1,388	30,139
Social Science	17,874	588	18,462
Personnel	2,576	314	2,890
Admin. Clerical	315,669	18,262	333,931
Biology	33,074	1,034	34,108
Accounting	39,986	2,148	42,134
Medical	139,231	891	140,122
Veterinary	2,718	8	2,726
Engineering	118,790	4,987	123,777
Legal	10,301	2,165	12,466
Information	14,828	2,782	17,610
Business	9,563	1,041	10,604
Physical	40,800	2,770	43,570
Library	5,902	3,237	9,139
Math	14,618	570	15,188
Equipment	17,012	559	17,571
Education	29,241	343	29,584
Supply	47,271	872	48,143
Transportation	14,383	276	14,659
All White Collar	902,588	44,234	946,822
All Blue Collar	413,251	4,654	417,905
All Positions	1,315,839	48,888	1,364,727

NOTE: HHS = Health and Human Services; GSA = General Services Administration; NASA = National Aeronautics and Space Administration; TVA = Tennessee Valley Authority.

COST-SAVINGS ESTIMATES

When the rates of cost reductions presented in the section on cost-savings rates (including both contracting and internal reorganization cost savings) are multiplied by the in-house expenditure figures presented in the section on expenditures on in-house commercial services, total potential cost savings from full consideration of increased competition can be calculated. The total annual potential cost-savings estimates are presented in Table 2.4.[24] The estimate based on the CBO's employment classification analysis is $16.6 billion annually, with $12.7 billion resulting from privatization, and $3.9 billion resulting from the reorganization caused by privatization reviews. These projections, like any others, are subject to the errors previously discussed, but provide a rough estimate of the upper limit of potential savings from fully expanded competition policies. Even if only one-third of these savings were realized, annual cost savings would still be $5.5 billion, with $4.2 billion attributable to privatization, and $1.3 billion attributable to reorganization savings.[25]

The estimated present value of a perpetual stream of annual potential savings of $5.5 billion to $16.6 billion is $61 billion to $184 billion.[26]

CONCLUSION

Competition between in-house and outside organizations to produce commercial services for the government has been part of federal government operations for many years under the A-76 program. Despite the several years of effort, relatively few federal operations have completed A-76 reviews. For those that have, the record of the effects on costs is striking. In the vast majority of cases, continuing over several years, A-76 competition studies resulted in substantial cost savings.

Table 2.3
Estimates of Cost Savings from Previous Studies

Organization	Initial Annual Expenditure per Position*	Annual Expected Savings per Position	Savings Rate
National Academy of Public Administration	$38,000	$3,800 to $5,700	10% to 15%
OMB	$23,923 to $35,885	$4,7846 to $7,177	20%
Grace Commission	$46,000 to $57,500	$9,200 to $11,500	20%
Heritage Found.	$20,000	$6,000	30%
Congressional Budget Office	$40,000	$12,000	30%

* Full-time-equivalent employee.

SOURCE: U.S. General Accounting Office (1986).

NOTE: The Office of Management and Budget (OMB) has used a 30% savings rate and cost savings per employee reviewed under A-76 of $10,000.

Table 2.4
**Estimated Annual Savings from Increasing Competition
in Federal Commercial Services**

Commercial Jobs Estimate	Total Budget Estimated Savings	% Cost Annual Cost Savings
1,400,000	$ 56 billion 30%*	$ 16.6 billion
1,400,000	$ 56 billion 10%	$ 5.6 billion

* The actual rate used is 29.75%, derived from 35% savings on 65% of the positions (contracted outside) and 20% on 35% of the positions (retained in-house after management improvements).

NOTE: All estimates assume an expenditure per position of $40,000 based on the Congressional Budget Office's estimates.

Some of these savings came from lower worker salaries or benefits; however, substantial real resource savings have also been obtained. These real resource savings have occurred both when the reviews resulted in contracts being let and when in-house units were competitive, retaining the work.

These findings are strongly consistent with the hypothesis that competition increases efficiency in providing commercial government services.

Estimates of total cost savings are subject to significant variability, but providing some reasonable range of estimated savings is an important task because it can signal to decision makers that it is worth their time and effort to consider this option more fully. Using the best available estimates, DOD's actual expenditure saving experience[27] and the CBO's review of position classifications, the estimated upper bound of potential expenditure savings from full implementation of privatization reviews is $16.6

billion annually, expressed in 1986 dollars. The lower bound estimate based on older studies is $5.5 billion annually.

ADDENDUM ON THE UNITED STATES POSTAL SERVICE

No overall detailed efficiency review of the United States Postal Service (USPS) has yet been undertaken, however, significant progress in that direction has recently been made under the auspices of the U.S. Postal Rate Commission.[28] Both the recent work and more limited research efforts and press reports dealing with the compensation of postal workers and other costs, prices, and quality measures have pointed toward substantial productivity problems in the USPS.[29] If rates of potential cost savings from increased competition are as high at the USPS as they are in other agencies, application of the A-76 review process in the USPS could provide substantial additional cost savings. Unfortunately, an equivalent break-out of USPS employees is not available from the CBO. However, other data for estimating potential budgetary cost savings from increased competition at the USPS are available.

Potential Cost Savings Calculated by Comparing Costs

Although there is continued debate about their proper interpretation, detailed statistical studies and a related literature suggests that the USPS provides a premium rate of compensation.[30] Average USPS compensation is estimated to be 21% above that of workers with similar skills. Independent inquiries provide some evidence that (1) federal postal workers have roughly similar pay scales for some job classifications,[31] but not for others,[32] (2) the USPS has a much larger proportion of higher classification workers assigned to mail sorting,[33] and (3) the USPS operates with a low capital to labor ratio compared to private delivery firms.[34] More recently, the U.S. Postal Rate Commission (PRC) staff studied the total factor productivity and labor productivity of the USPS relative that of the U.S. manufacturing sector. The staff of the PRC found that productivity improvement at the USPS have been far smaller than those in manufacturing generally. Between 1971 and 1987, USPS labor productivity in mail processing rose 11.7% compared to a 54.6% increase in labor productivity in manufacturing.   At the same time USPS compensation rose 6.7% in real terms while manufacturing real wages fell.[35]

Using the 21% compensation premium and an estimate that 83% of USPS costs are for labor, the potential annual cost savings from equalizing compensation levels with private mail firms would be $6 billion annually in current dollars.[36] The savings in this case might represent income redistribution back to mailers and consumers from USPS workers rather than real resource savings.[37]

Using cost reduction estimates based on reported savings rates from contracting out USPS delivery routes, the Cato Institute estimated potential cost reductions of $12 billion annually in operating the postal system competitively.[38]

Potential Costs Savings Calculated by Comparing Prices

Both private and public firms provide mail delivery services, albeit for somewhat different types of items.[39] Given the similarity in the functions carried out by the public and private mail delivery services, comparative cost trends can be assessed, assuming stable profit levels. When price changes for public and private firms are compared, public mail prices have increased much more.[40] If prices for private and public mail service could be made to be equivalent through increased competition, it has been estimated that as much as $12 billion in annual savings to consumers could result.[41]

Quality Comparisons

The USPS has established performance benchmarks for itself. Considerable evidence is available indicating that the USPS does not meet its own service standards. Further, official measurements of its performance are questionable.[42]

Consumer patronage of the USPS is another possible measure of quality of service, although price clearly is a major consideration as well. In some areas, the USPS acts as a statutory monopolist so patronage measurements are not meaningful. In other areas, however, the USPS directly competes with private mail services. In each one of these, private firms have taken more than 80% of sales. Competitive services include parcel post, expedited mail, and electronic mail. Between 1967 and 1987, the USPS's parcel post volume *declined* 80% primarily due to competition from UPS.[43] In expedited mail, USPS's share has declined dramatically due to competition from private firms, especially the innovative services offered by Federal Express. In electronic mail, USPS was forced to exit from the business.

Conclusion

Conceptually, there is no apparent reason to exclude the postal service from A-76 reviews. The USPS is not an inherently governmental function (at least at the current stage of technological development where numerous alternative methods of communication to "tie" the various regions of the country together are readily available) and private delivery firms that could compete is supplying postal services are numerous.[44] Further there is no reason to believe that A-76 reviews in the USPS would provide less savings than reviews in other parts of the government. The empirical evidence suggests that significant expenditure savings, ranging between $6 and $12 billion annually, would be possible through increased competition. There is less evidence available about the extent of potential productivity improvements.

NOTES

1. Civilian compensation of $71 billion plus $147 billion in purchases other than military procurement totals to $218 billion.

2. The estimated cost savings calculated in this study do not include government budget reductions from privatization through complete service shedding; i.e., the service is no longer financed by the government after the government stops producing the service in-house.   There is no aggregate data available on these budget reductions and no data is available to assess costs to consumers of the private replacement, if any.

3. Governments as well as consumers are concerned about both price and quality of services. Hence, neither government nor consumers will always favor a decline in costs, if it results in a decline in quality of service.

4. See also, Stolzenberg and Berry (1985).

For a historical review of Circular A-76, see U.S. General Accounting Office (1978, pp. 5-12).   This report notes that A-76 contracting out experiences have been scrutinized extensively.   For example, the U.S. General Accounting Office (GAO) published over ninety reports on A-76 issues between 1972 and 1978 (U.S. General Accounting Office, 1978, pp. 130-40.)

5. Musell (1987).

6. Without this internal reassessment of in-house production techniques, in-house cost estimates used in A-76 reviews would be higher.

7. A standard comparing current costs to private contract costs would result in a higher percentage of activities being privatized. Experience at the Department of Defense suggests, however, that projected internal savings from reorganization are usually realized (Musell, 1987, p. 6).

8. See the President's Commission on Privatization (1988, pp. 134-36).   The General Accounting Office made similar findings in the late 1970s (U.S. General Accounting Office, 1981a). During the late 1980s, the OMB established an office specifically to encourage agencies to comply with Circular A-76, and Executive Order 12615 was directed at increasing agency participation.   About $40 billion is now spent for external procurement of commercial services (including both defense and nondefense agencies), but much of this is for construction work and other services that are not part of the A-76 program.

Part of the reason for the DOD's strong interest in A-76 may stem from its authorization to reprogram cost savings into other DOD activities.

9. Musell (1987).

10. Discussed below.

11. Musell (1987).

12. This cost-saving rate could possibly be improved if provisions in the Service Contract Act of 1965 were modified to allow contractors to offer lower wages for construction helpers (currently, helpers must receive

journeyman's wages) and wages lower than the average in the area where the contractor operates. The estimated cost savings from this change in construction projects, for example, is approximately $170 million annually, about 3% to 4% of total expenditures for construction projects covered by the Act (U.S. Congressional Budget Office, 1988, pp. 252-53). Relaxation of additional provisions of the act might be expected to provide additional total cost savings, but CBO has not estimated the extent of such potential savings.

13. The new government retirement plan reduces the government's contribution toward retirement.

14. The reasons for increases in contract costs have been a source of controversy and this CBO adjustment is designed to incorporate these concerns. The ideal method for assessing cost savings is to compare actual contract costs to the costs that would have occurred if the function had remained in-house. The simplest way to accomplish this might be to assume that government costs would have increased at the same rate as contract costs. However, some evidence disputes this. This CBO adjustment accommodates this concern by reducing the rate used to inflate in-house costs from old dollars.

Some commentators on contracting under A-76 have suggested that actual contract costs have inflated faster than government costs because of postcontractual opportunistic behavior of contractors (AFSCME, 1983, 1988). However, in the types of relatively well defined and readily monitored services being discussed here, the probability of successful postcontractual opportunistic behavior should be small.

To address this question empirically, detailed studies of contract cost increases in the A-76 program have been conducted. These reviews have generally concluded that contract costs often do increase faster than inflation, but these increases are generally small and often relate to changes in contract terms requested by the government or to relatively higher wage increases required by Davis Bacon regulations. On occasion, contract costs have increased because the contract had to be rebid because of default by the original contractor, but these circumstances are rare and usually the new contract continues to offer savings relative to in-house production. The CBO study, which examined the widest sample of DOD contracts, found that after one year or more of operation, actual cost savings amounted to 96% of originally estimated costs savings. Similar "realization ratios" have been observed in in-house reorganizations stemming from A-76 studies; that is, the actual cost savings from reorganizing in-house production closely match projected savings made during the review process even without controlling for the fact that inflation affects actual contract costs but not the original in-house cost estimates. Thus, these studies generally confirm the integrity of the original A-76 cost-savings estimates.

15. U.S. GAO (1986, pp. 10-5).

16. Personal communication with A-76 officials at OMB, 1987-1988.

17. The author wishes to thank the staff of CBO for suggesting these words of caution in interpreting the cost-savings estimates.

18. Expenditures for positions includes both personnel costs and average materials and equipment costs associated with these positions.

19. A detailed program evaluation will involve classification of individual tasks, such as secretarial support or maintenance of the motor vehicle fleet. These task categories closely parallel the occupational categories in a personnel classification analysis.

20. Musell (1987).

21. This estimate excludes the U.S. Postal Service. If the postal service is included, the figure rises to approximately 2.1 million workers out of a total of 3.1 million civilian employees of the federal government (*World Almanac and Book of Facts 1988*, 1988, p. 85).

22. Musell (1987, p. 17). Employment calculations are done on a FTE basis to avoid biases that might arise if agencies differed in the proportion of part-time personnel they employed.

23. As the 1986 GAO report *Federal Productivity* states, "[t]he estimates (of cost savings from privatization) differ primarily because of different assumptions regarding the number of white collar, commercial-type positions that would be studied," (U.S. GAO, 1986, p. 10). The estimates of commercial activities (potentially suitable for outside production) prior to the CBO's study had a narrower scope of concern than the present study, namely savings that could be obtained in the near future or savings that could be obtained without ending exemptions from the A-76 process. The estimates from these earlier studies ranged from 418,000 to 1,000,000 positions. The CBO, however, based its estimates on a broader concern, namely, the overall long-run maximum potential of increased competition, which is also the focus of this study.

24. The CBO's own cost-savings estimates were limited to three options within a five-year time horizon that envisioned utilizing current in-house program analysis capabilities of the executive departments and envisioned continuation of the congressional exemptions that exclude A-76 studies of many government services, for example, roughly 275,000 civilian DOD positions and most Veterans Administration and Park Service positions (Musell, 1987, pp. 11-12, 22-26).

25. The CBO's estimate is the best available estimate. The cost-savings estimate of 10%, one-third of the CBO's rate, was suggested by

the National Academy of Public Administration (see Table 2.3) without the benefit of recent data from A-76 studies.

26. Based on a 9% discount rate.

27. DOD's estimates are reduced as suggested by the CBO to take into account recent changes in pensions and cost-of-living pay adjustments in the federal government.

28. The USPS let a contract for an overall assessment of methods to increase its efficiency. The USPS projects cost savings from this effort of approximately $3 to $4 billion. The contract, however, has been questioned by Congress and has been the subject of litigation and delay (Schmid, 1988).

The Department of Justice (DOJ) undertook research concerning the costs of the USPS. The DOJ research was part of an effort to assess potential privatization options. Work on the project was abandoned at the end of President Reagan's term of office.

A recent report by the U.S. Postal Rate Commission Staff (1990) sought to remedy the lack of overall productivity information. The Postal Rate Commission staff found that measurements of productivity growth undertaken by the management of the USPS during the 1980s were seriously overstated because they failed to account for shifts in the mix of mail.

29. See, for example, Bandow (1990) and Matlock (1988).

30. In particular, see Adie (1977) and Perloff and Wachter (1984). See Sorkin (1980) for a general discussion of wage premium evidence. Asher and Popkin (1984), on the other hand, attribute higher costs to less race and sex discrimination in the U.S. Postal Service.

A number of criticisms can be raised to this justification of the wage premiums paid by the postal service. First, law enforcement against racial discrimination may be a less costly method of providing nondiscriminatory job opportunities. Second, the USPS should not have to pay premium wage rates to attract sufficient qualified workers. Quit rates are extremely low (Perloff and Wachter, 1984, pp. 31-32.) Third, the USPS has sought to negotiate lower entry level wages in acknowledgement that USPS wages are higher than comparable wages in business and other areas of government. See Adie (1989). Finally, although Perloff and Wachter (1984) find a significant race effect in modeling wages levels, there is no significant race-industry interaction term once education and experiences are controlled for.

31. Private sector couriers and USPS carriers have similar wage levels.

32. The U.S. General Accounting Office (1982b) reported that janitors employed by the USPS were paid more than twice the rate of their counterparts outside the government.

33. Telephone conversations with staff of the Postal Rate Commission and Federal Express, November 1987.

34. MacAvoy and McIsaac (1987). MacAvoy and McIsaac also provide efficiency evidence comparing government and private enterprises in other services. Also see Boardman and Vining (1989).

35. See U.S. Postal Rate Commission Staff (1990, pp. 74-100).

36. President's Commission on Privatization (1988, pp. 112-16).

37. Real resource savings could result if the high wages in the USPS attract more productive workers to the USPS who are underutilized by the USPS. If this is the case, increasing competition in the USPS could save resources by releasing these more productive workers to the rest of the economy where they would be better utilized.

38. Bovard (1990). The fact that substantial savings rates have been obtained in contracting rural routes suggests that increased competition could be utilized in much of the system. Supporters of a monopolized postal service have frequently cited assumed difficulties in attracting private delivery firms to service rural routes.

These cost-savings estimates do not include gains in allocative efficiency that could result from pricing postal services closer to their marginal social cost.

39. Efforts continue to evaluate coverage of the postal monopoly statutes. Recently, for example, third class mail users have sought to obtain an exemption for addressed third class mail. See Hilke and Vita (1989).

40. Although price performance of the USPS is not good in comparison to private mail delivery firms, its price performance is quite good compared to prices in the Canadian postal service (Stanbury, 1987, pp. 42-52).

41. MacAvoy and McIsaac (1987). Their estimate is completely independent of the Cato Institute's estimate cited earlier.

42. Bovard (1990). See also, Green (1986, p. 74); Blyskal and Hodge (1987, pp. 43-55); and Adie (1987).

43. U.S. Postal Service (1987a, p. III-1).

44. Security and secrecy of government communications are also no longer a convincing argument for government production of postal services. Alternative forms of secure communication are available and are widely used by government and private parties. Further, private firms competing with the postal service (in expedited mail, parcel delivery, and courier services, for example) are also apparently able to offer

assurances to mailers that materials will remain secure from theft or tampering during shipment.

3

Local Government
Potential Cost Savings

INTRODUCTION

Local governments[1] and states provide a wide variety of services and consequently constitute a significant segment of the economy. On average, state and local governments spent over $2,000 per capita on current goods and services, or a total of over $500 billion in 1986, a third more than the federal government.[2] These average figures subsume immense variations in both the levels of spending and in the types of services performed.

Local and state government activities, like those in the federal government, conceptually can be divided into inherently governmental functions and commercial functions. Commercial services, corresponding to private goods in cells II and IV in Figure 1.1 and some public goods in cell I, could be supplied by private firms (or other government agencies) either on a contract basis or through some other competitive format without severe delegation of power problems. In parallel with the discussion in chapter 2, inherently governmental services include those with extensive discretion or policy impact. For this reason, judicial, legislative, and police functions are usually regarded as inherently governmental and will be deemphasized here,[3] although some methods for increasing competition may be effectively applied to aspects of these services as well. Commercial activities are not inherently governmental and several private commercial firms or other outside organizations are frequently well positioned to compete in supplying these services to government.

Efforts to reduce state and local government costs grew substantially when limitations on government revenue sources, such as Proposition 13 in California, became widespread in the late 1970s and early 1980s. Another contributing factor was the decline in federal aid to local governments.[4]

As discussed in the previous chapter, creating potential total cost-savings estimates requires information on the (1) rate of cost savings and (2) total expenditures on in-house commercial services, where increased competition might be introduced successfully in the future. Producing such estimates for local and state governments is the objective of this chapter.

For state and local governments, the best available sources of information on the rate of cost savings come from studies of cost savings focused on individual government services. The studies reviewed in this chapter focus primarily on competitive contracting with for-profit private firms, but intergovernmental and interagency competition studies are also included.[5]

The best available source of data on total expenditures on in-house commercial services is the *Census of Governments* (U.S. Department of Commerce, Bureau of the Census, 1988, 1987).[6] This data is available on a program-by-program basis.[7]

Data for some expenditure categories covered in the census are not included in the cost-savings estimates here. In some instances, there are few if any studies that closely match the expenditure category. No total cost-savings estimates are produced for these categories, since there appears to be an insufficient basis for making cost-savings estimates. Similarly, expenditure categories where empirical studies have reached diametrically opposite conclusions, and no resolution of the differences has been obtained, are not included. The most prominent budget category of this kind is education.[8] Finally, expenditure categories that are widely believed to involve inherently governmental activities are not included.[9] These services include police protection, the courts, tax collection, regulatory agencies, and law-making and policy analysis.

Equation (1) shows the calculation for separating expenditures in the two groups of jurisdictions, those with in-house monopolies and those with various forms of increased competition:

(1) $T = (1 - m)(1 - s)P + mP,$

where T is total expenditures for a particular service summed across all jurisdictions, m is the proportion of jurisdictions that continue to have in-house monopoly production, s is the rate of total cost savings in the jurisdictions that have implemented techniques to increase competition, and P is the total expenditures that would pertain if there were no cost savings from increased competition.

In equation (1), the first set of terms to the right of the equal sign (and to the left of the addition sign) gives expenditures in jurisdictions with increased competition whereas the second set of terms gives expenditures in the in-house monopoly jurisdictions.

Solving equation (1) for P yields equation (2).

(2) $P = T / (1 - s + ms).$

Substituting equation (2) back into the second set of terms in equation (1), gives equation (3) for the total expenditures in the in-house monopoly jurisdictions, E:

(3) $E = mT / (1 - s + ms).$

Cost savings from increased competition, S, is then sE, the rate of cost savings times expenditures in in-house monopoly jurisdictions. This is shown in equation (4):

(4) $S = smT / (1 - s + ms) = sE.$[10]

RATES OF POTENTIAL TOTAL COST SAVINGS

As discussed above, the first necessary component for calculating cost savings is a set of rate-of-savings estimates, s in the equations above. For local and state governments, the best sources of estimates of total cost-savings rates are studies of individual local and state services where increased competition has been introduced.[11]

The Stevens Study

There are many studies of cost savings from increased competition in individual services and, as will be shown, the vast majority of them find that increased competition can provide substantial rates of cost savings in the 20% to 50% range. However, research that includes detailed direct evaluations of service quality, community characteristics, and technology is scarce because it is extremely costly to develop the necessary data.[12] One effect of this scarcity is to underscore the importance of the few detailed studies that are available, because they can serve to validate the plausibility of other studies finding similar cost-savings rates.

Perhaps the most widely referenced, detailed study of cost savings and of changes in service quality from increased competition is a 1984 study by Stevens.[13]   This study, sponsored by the Department of Housing and Urban Development, found total cost savings, associated with increased competition, of 20% to 50% for seven of eight services studied. The Stevens study also found that, although the proportions differ in different services, less than 40% of the average total cost reductions were due to differences in compensation.[14]

To examine the effects of increased competition on local government costs, the Stevens study identified a single geographic area where a sizable proportion of municipal services are produced on a contract basis by private for-profit firms.[15]   Next, local government services were reviewed to determine which services were provided both by in-house monopoly agencies and by contractors in enough cities to provide a reasonable sample. Eight services met all of the criteria. These services are street cleaning, janitorial services, residential refuse collection, payroll processing, traffic signal maintenance, asphalt overlay construction, turf maintenance, and street tree maintenance.

Having selected the services to be studied, Stevens and her research team then constructed two samples of ten municipalities for each separate service. Cities in one group used an monopoly in-house agency to produce the service. Cities in the second sample used a contractor. The cities were matched, to the maximum extent possible, with respect to size, average income, and other characteristics. Both selecting a single geographic area and employing a matched sample design are techniques used to hold constant a number of alternative explanatory factors that may be difficult to observe or quantify. These controls decrease the number of cities (i.e., the sample size) needed to find statistically significant results and help ensure that miscellaneous, but hard to quantify, differences between regions are not responsible for cost differences between cities.

After the sample of cities was selected, measures of the level (amount) of service and quality of the service were constructed and data were collected. Detailed data on costs and community characteristics were also gathered along with information on management and production techniques (types of equipment used, for example).

The data on costs and characteristics were analyzed using several different statistical methods ranging from simply comparing average costs to more sophisticated techniques (i.e., multiple regression analysis) designed to take account of many observed characteristics expected to affect costs. Finally, results from the various statistical tests were considered together in reaching a final evaluation of cost differences and explanations for these cost differences. Part of this evaluation considered how low-cost jurisdictions differed from high-cost jurisdictions, holding constant the degree of outside contracting.

As an example of the detailed and direct observation techniques used in measuring technology, community characteristics, and service quality in the Stevens study, Appendix B condenses the methodology section in the Stevens study's analysis of turf maintenance services. The elements in the analysis include: definition of turf maintenance activities; review of alternative technologies and items of equipment; development of output, cost, and quality measures; description of characteristics of the sample cities; analysis of cost differences between in-house monopoly agencies and contract providers using pooled data;[16] and analysis of cost differences using matched pair analysis.[17]

Table 3.1a summarizes the cost savings observed on each service studied by Stevens.[18] By way of illustration, Table 3.1b presents the main findings on service quality and explanations for cost differences between in-house monopoly agencies and contract providers for street cleaning. Summary findings for the other services studied are listed in the Appendix C.

In each service except payroll processing, cities with contract providers had at least 20% lower costs, on average, than cities with monopoly in-house production, after a wide range of differences in city characteristics are controlled for.[19] The smallest average cost difference observed, aside from payroll, was for refuse collection. The weighted average cost saving from privatization, including all of the services and cities studied, was 27.4%. There were no significant differences in the level of quality of service in any of the services studied.[20]

In addition to analyzing each service separately, the Stevens study also pooled the entire sample of services. After standardizing across measures and conducting matched pair and regression analyses, the authors confirmed their findings on individual services and concluded that contract services are provided at lower cost with no sacrifice of quality.[21]

Other Studies

The estimated cost reductions found in the Stevens study are generally consistent with findings from other independent comparisons of the costs of in-house government agencies versus private commercial producers.

Table 3.2 updates and expands an earlier compilation of cost studies.[22] It references over one hundred independent studies of increased competition in individual government services (both national and local government services) and the cost differences observed. The studies are categorized by the service being analyzed. Studies that obtained quantitative results typically found cost reductions of 20% to 50% that resulted from increased competition.[23]

Although contracting out is the predominant method of increasing competition in the collection of studies, it is not the only avenue examined in the literature. Results from two widely recognized alternative methods of increasing competition are also included in Table 3.2.

Table 3.1a
Stevens Study Findings - Percentage Cost Savings,
Holding Other Factors Constant

Service	Rate of Cost Savings*
Street Cleaning	30.1%
Janitorial Services	42.2%
Refuse Collection (residential)	21.9%
Payroll Processing	0.0%
Traffic Signal Maintenance	35.9%
Asphalt Overlay	49.0%
Turf Maintenance	28.6%
Street Tree Maintenance	27.0%

* Calculated as (Municipal Agency Costs - Contract City Costs) / Municipal Agency Costs.

SOURCE: Stevens (1984)

The first alternative involves inviting management and workers of the in-house monopoly agency to bid against private contract bidders. This is essentially the same process utilized in the A-76 program in the federal government. The most notable example of competition between private and public bidders is found in Phoenix, Arizona, where the practice began in the mid-1970s.

The Phoenix system involves a modified competitive sealed bid. Both private contractors and a city department interested in obtaining a contract with the city submit sealed bids. Before the city department can submit its bid, however, a special bid-auditing department established by the city has to certify that the service really could be provided in-house for the amount of the proposed bid.[24] The contract is awarded to the lowest bidder, with a small (3%) preference given to the city agency if it is the incumbent contractor. City agencies have been successful bidders on several occasions and recently have won a large proportion of the bids that the city has let.[25]

Table 3.1b
Main Quality of Service Findings and Reasons for Observed Cost Differences in the Stevens Study of Street Cleaning

---

*   The quality of service provided by contractors and municipal agencies is almost identical. On a four point rating scale, with 1 = cleanest and 4 = dirtiest, observers, on average, rated contract cities as 1.62 and municipal cities as 1.66.

*   Most of the difference in the cost of contract as compared to municipal street cleaning appears to be explained by four factors: (1) speed and duration of sweeping -- contract crews sweep more miles per shift hour and work longer shifts than do municipal crews; (2) management and fringe benefits -- contractors achieve a much lower absentee rate (which here defines vacation absences as an absence) than do municipalities; (3) supervision of workers -- contractors have a much wider span of control for workers than do municipalities; and (4) responsibility for equipment maintenance -- contractors are more likely to be responsible for equipment maintenance than are the municipal departments delivering street cleaning services.

SOURCE: Stevens (1984).

A variant of the Phoenix procedure is used in Minneapolis, where private refuse collection firms compete to serve part of the city, while the rest is reserved for the in-house refuse agency. However, the city makes aggressive use of the cost information about private contractors to create a yardstick for the in-house agency. Over the years, the in-house agency's higher costs have gradually been reduced to the level of the private contractors.[26]

The second contractual arrangement for increasing competition involves intergovernmental contracting.   Intergovernmental contracting is an agreement between two or more jurisdictions in which one jurisdiction drops in-house production and purchases the service from another government. Competition occurs between in-house agencies in all the jurisdictions that might contract with each other.

Table 3.2
Updated Cost Savings Research Findings
Arranged Alphabetically by Service Category

Source[27]	Comparison	Findings

1. Airline Operation and Airplane Maintenance:

Savas (1987)	In-house versus contract maintenance support for air force bases.	Contract maintenance reduced costs by 13% while improving availability of parts and planes. Cost savings were primarily attributable to use of 25% fewer personnel by contractors.
Davies (1971, 1977)	Australia/sole private airline versus its lone public counterpart.	Efficiency indices of private airline were 12% to 100% higher.
Domberger and Piggott (1986)	Survey article dealing with many services. Focus on Australian airlines.	Concludes that private firms are generally more efficient, unless the public firms are faced with equivalent competition.

2. Airports:

Auditor General of Canada (1985)	Tax supported Canadian airport operations versus comparable U.S. airport authorities that must borrow in capital markets to finance their facilities.	Airports subject to capital market discipline are much more efficient. Workyear requirements are 30% to 40% lower. Canadian government workers have inflexible work assignments and procedures. Canadian airports are overbuilt and neglect many commercial opportunities. Fail to monitor trends in operating costs. Overall savings rate is 40%.

Table 3.2 (continued)

Source	Comparison	Findings
Moore (1987)	In-house versus contract air-traffic control.	Contracting saves 25% to 50%.
Roth (1987)	Government managed versus private managed airports.	Government pricing policies for landing rights and other airport services lead to inefficient congestion and inability to finance expansion of facilities.

3. <u>All Services</u>:

Deacon (1979)	In-house versus intergovernmental production of all services.	Intergovernmental contracting saved 14% relative to in-house production.
David (1987)	In-house versus private contracted services.	Surveyed local administrators reported that cost savings were, achieved in 98% of contracting efforts. The range of operating cost savings was large: 10% reported more than 40% savings. The weighted average cost saving was 19%.
Savas (1987)	Los Angeles county in-house services versus contracted services from 1979 to 1984.	Cost of contracted services averaged 30% less than in-house services.
Moore (1987)	In-house versus contract in Mirada, California.	Contracting has 30% lower costs.

Table 3.2 (continued)

Source	Comparison	Findings

4. Assessment, Property Tax (financial administration) - also see Payroll and Data Processing (service category 28):

Stocker (1973)	In-house versus private contractors in Ohio.	Private assessments provided 50% cost savings and were found to be more accurate.

5. Banks:

Davies (1982)	Australia/one public versus one private bank.	Sign and magnitude of all indices of productivity, responsiveness to risk, and profitability favor private banks.

6. Bus Service (utilities) - also see Electric Utilities and Water Utilities (service categories 10 and 43):

Morlok and Moseley (1986)	Municipal in-house agency versus competitive contracts.	Contract winners supplied services at 28% lower costs.
Morlok and Viton (1985)	Municipal in-house agency versus contracts awarded in competitive bidding versus noncompetitive contracts.	Contract providers had costs 50% to 60% lower than municipal agencies they replaced. Noncompetitive contracts were similar to municipal agency costs.
Oelert (1976)	Municipal in-house versus private bus service in W. Germany.	Public bus services have 160% higher costs per kilometer than private equivalents.
Walters (1987)	Municipal in-house versus private bus service in various cities.	Private bus services typically charge similar prices, but have 50% to 65% lower costs.

Table 3.2 (continued)

Source	Comparison	Findings
Perry and Babitsky (1986)	Private versus cost plus contract versus municipal in-house versus regional in-house authority bus operators.	Private operators are significantly more efficient. Cost-plus contractors and municipal bus lines are less efficient. Inefficient private operators are sold to government.
Pomme-rehne and Schneider (1985)	In-house versus private firms in West Germany.	Private costs were 60% lower than public costs for commercial bus operations.
Talley and Anderson (1986)	In-house motor bus versus contracted dial-a-ride service.	Substituting dial-a-ride for scheduled service decreased costs by reducing overtime and idle time and utilizing less costly vehicles. It also reduced costs indirectly by encouraging competition with traditional services of the agency.
Teal, Guiliano, and Morlok (1986)	In-house versus competitive contract operators.	Competitive contract operations provided cost savings from 10% to 50% (larger fleets). Cost savings are due both to less overhead/greater productivity and lower wages.
Rice Center (1985)	In-house versus contract express commuter services.	Contract operators have 30% to 60% lower costs..

Table 3.2 (continued)

Source	Comparison	Findings

7. Cleaning Services (general maintenance of public buildings) - also see Security Services (service catetory 37):

Source	Comparison	Findings
Bundesrech nungshof (1972)	In-house versus private contracting of cleaning services in West German post offices.	In-house service 40% to 60% more costly
Hamburger Senat (1974), Fischer-Menshau-sen (1975)	In-house versus private contracting out in West German public buildings.	Public service 50% more costly than private alternative.
Kaiser (1977)	In-house versus con-tract services in schools.	Contracting saved 13.4% of costs.
Pomme-rehne and Schneider (1985)	In-house versus private sector costs of services in West Germany.	Private costs were 33% lower than public costs for commercial cleaning services.
U.S. GAO (1981b)	In-house staff versus GSA contractors versus private landlords.	Private window cleaning costs averaged 47% lower than GSA staff while contractors costs were 38% lower costs. Higher costs were due to higher wages as well as more workers.
Stevens (1984)	In-house versus contract janitorial services.	Contract service had 42% lower costs even after accounting for quality, service levels, and economies of scale.

Table 3.2 (continued)

Source	Comparison	Findings
U.S. GAO (1982b), Fixler and Poole (1987)	In-house versus contracted janitorial services in post offices.	Contracted janitorial services were 50% less costly than in-house services.

8. Day Care Centers:

Bennett and DiLorenzo (1983)	In-house versus private providers of equivalent services. Article is based on GAO studies.	Private day care was found to be 45% less costly because of fewer teachers, lower wages, and fewer nonteaching staff.

9. Debt Collection:

Bennett & DiLorenzo (1983)	In-house versus private providers of equivalent services.	Private debt collection procedures were faster and 60% less costly.
Bennett & Johnson (1980)	In-house versus privately contracted equivalent services.	Government 200% more costly per dollar of debt pursued.

10. Electric Utilities (utilities) - also see Bus Services and Water Utilities (service categories 6 and 43):

Bennett & DiLorenzo (1983)	In-house federal agencies versus private hydroelectric plants.	Private utility costs averaged 17% lower due primarily to federal overstaffing.
Hellman (1972)	In-house versus electric utilities that compete versus regulated private monopolies.	Competition produced lower rates than regulation. Government production produced the lowest rates, due to tax exemptions.

Table 3.2 (continued)

Source	Comparison	Findings
Meyer (1975)	In-house versus private firms, sample of sixty to ninety U.S. utilities.	Slightly higher costs of private production. Threat of competition improved cost efficiency somewhat.
Moore (1970)	In-house versus private U.S. utilities.	Overcapitalization greater in public firms. Total operating costs of public firms higher.
Primeaux (1975)	In-house monopoly versus in-house operations that compete with private firms.	Municipal utilities facing competition have 11% lower costs on average. Economies of scale offset X-inefficiency at big firms.
Spann (1977)	In-house versus private firms in Texas and California.	Private firms, adjusted for scale, are as or more efficient in operating cost and investment.
Atkinson and Halvorsen (1986)	U.S. public utilities.	Public utilities are as efficient as private utilities.
Wallace and Junck (1970)	In-house versus private firms by region of the U.S.	Operating costs 40% to 75% higher in public mode. Investment is 40% higher (per kilowatt) in public mode.
Bellamy (1981)	Monopoly versus competing utilities.	Competing utilities had 20% lower prices.

Financial Administration: See Assessment, Property Tax (service category 4) and Payroll and Data Processing (service category 28).

Table 3.2 (continued)

Source	Comparison	Findings
11. Fire Protection:		
Ahlbrandt (1973, 1974), Moore (1988)	In-house (Seattle) versus private (Scottsdale, Arizona).	Municipal fire departments 39% to 88% higher cost per capita.
Hilke (1986)	In-house versus varying degrees of use of volunteers in New York and Pennsylvania cities (not suburbs) with populations between 10,000 and 50,000.	Use of volunteers reduced firefighting costs. Cities in New York with all-volunteer departments had 62% lower costs per capita. Pennsylvania's all-volunteer cities saved an average of 79% per capita. A 10% increase in use of volunteers provides a 2.8% decrease in costs.
Kristensen (1983)	In-house versus major private provider in Denmark.	The principal private firm provided services at 65% lower costs. Differences in costs due to economies of scale, lower input costs, and especially part-time reservists and lower X-inefficiencies.
McDavid and Butler (1984)	In-house versus in-house/volunteer services in Canada.	Mixed fire departments averaged 33% lower costs than purely municipal departments.
Poole (1976), Smith (1983)	Private versus contract fire fighting.	Switching to private contract fire fighting reduces costs by 20% to 50%.

Table 3.2 (continued)

Source	Comparison	Findings

12. Forestry:

Bundesregi erung Deutsch- land (1976)	In-house versus private in West Germany.	Annual operating revenues 45 DM per hectare higher in private forests (approximately $6 per acre).
Pfister (1976)	In-house versus private in the state of Baden- Wurttemberg, Germany.	Labor input twice as high per unit of output in public as compared with private firms.

General Maintenance of Public Buildings: See Cleaning Services (service category 7) and Security Services (service category 37).

13. Health Services - also see Nursing Homes (service category 25):

Schle-sing, Dorwart, and Pulice (1986)	In-house versus contract mental health services.	Nominally competitive contracting procedure resulted in sole source supply with little increase in efficiency.
Valente and Man- chester (1984)	In-house supply of substance abuse programs versus volunteer-based program.	Systematic volunteer program allowed service expansion with cost savings to the community.

14. Highways:

Deacon (1979)	In-house (local) versus intergovern-mental provision of street repair.	Intergovernmental contracting saved 30%.

Table 3.2 (continued)

Source	Comparison	Findings
Stevens (1984)	In-house versus contract provision of asphalt overlay and traffic light maintenance.	Contracting out was half as costly with equivalent quality. Contractors used more experienced staff and more equipment. Cost savings in the traffic light maintenance averaged 36%.

15. <u>Hospitals</u>:

Source	Comparison	Findings
Lindsay (1975)	In-house Veterans Administration (VA) versus private.	VA hospitals have lower costs and lower quality. Resource use is distorted toward outputs that are easily monitored by Congress. Actual costs per medically necessary hospital stay may be higher in VA hospitals after controlling for length of stay.
Robinson and Luft (1988)	Investor owned versus public hospitals using a sample of 5,490 hospitals.	Cost increases at public hospitals were 15% lower than those in investor-owned hospitals from 1982 to 1986 after controlling for various demand and cost factors.
Becker and Sloan (1985)	Investor-owned versus nonfederal government hopitals.	Government hospitals had no higher costs per admission.
Shortell and Hughes (1988)	Investor-owned versus nonfederal government versus nonprofit private hospitals.	No differences in quality, measured in death rates between different types of hospitals.

Table 3.2 (continued)

Source	Comparison	Findings
Register and Bruning (1987)	Investor-owned versus thirty-six nonfederal state and local government owned and operated hospitals.	No signficant efficiency differences between types after controlling for size and other factors that should effect efficiency.
Granne-mann, Brown, and Pauly (1986)	Investor-owned versus nonfederal government hospitals using a national sample of short-term hospitals.	Investor-owned hospitals had 24% higher costs than nonfederal government hospitals.
Noether (1987)	Investor-owned versus nonprofit hospitals including nonfederal government hospitals sampled from 223 metropolitan areas.	Investor-owned hospitals are significantly more efficient once tax payments are taken into consideration.
Lindsay (1976)	In-house Veterans Administration versus private.	Cost per patient day less in VA hospital, unadjusted for type of care and quality. Less "serious" cases and longer patient stays were observed in the VA facilities. The VA had a higher proportion of minority group professionals compared to proprietary hospitals.
Benton (1979)	In-house versus private home care.	Government had 43% lower cost. No controls for quality were made in the study.

Table 3.2 (continued)

Source	Comparison	Findings
Wilson and Jadlow (1978)	In-house versus private in 1,200 U.S. hospitals providing nuclear medicine services.	Proprietary hospitals more efficient than public hospitals.
Hatry (1983)	In-house managements versus contract management.	Experience with contract managements has varied. Seven out of fifteen large California public hospitals signing new management contracts with private management firms between 1973 and 1980 terminated the contracts. The hospitals noted small savings, service problems, and the hospital's ability to learn and then duplicate the cost-saving management techniques of private contractors.

16. Housing and Community Development:

Muth (1973)	In-house versus private construction costs in U.S. cities.	Public agencies 20% more costly per constant quality housing unit.
Rechnungs-hof Rhein-land Pfalz (1972)	In-house versus private cost of supplying large public projects in West Germany.	Public agencies 20% more costly than private contracting.

Table 3.2 (continued)

Source	Comparison	Findings
Schneider and Schuppener (1971)	In-house versus private construction in West Germany.	Public firms significantly more expensive suppliers.
Pommerehne and Schneider (1985)	In-house versus private costs in West Germany.	Private costs were lower than public costs for commercial services generally, 17% for construction.
President's Commission on Privatization (1988)	Publicly constructed versus various privatization alternatives.	Public housing costs per unit over twenty years total $69,863 versus $27,892 to obtain private units through housing subsidies to individual needy families.
Weicher (1980)	Government-financed construction versus private.	Government-financed construction 25% more costly. Government management is also more costly.

17. Insurance Claims Processing:

Hsiao (1978)	In-house versus private.	Equivalent claims processing costs of private insurers were between 15% and 26% lower. Most of the differences were attributable to compensation and organizational differences. Some cost differences were attributable to efforts by public insurance programs to control medical costs generally.

Table 3.2 (continued)

Source	Comparison	Findings
18. Insurance Sales and Servicing:		
Finsinger (1981)	In-house (five firms) versus private (seventy-seven firms) liability and life coverage in West Germany.	Competition between public and private firms prompted equivalent efficiency.
Kennedy and Mehr (1977)	In-house (in Manitoba) versus private (in Alberta).	Private insurance quality and service higher than those of the public insurance with equivalent costs.
19. Laundry Service:		
Pomme-rehne and Schneider (1985)	In-house versus private in West Germany.	Private costs were 46% lower than public costs for commercial services in laundry services.
20. Legal Services:		
Houlden and Balkin (1985)	Ordered assigned counsel versus contract counsel for indigents.	Contract counsel had at least 50% lower costs. Contract counsel processed cases in half the time of assigned counsel. The authors note that since fees per hour are roughly equal, the primary difference is due to less attorney time per case under the contract system. This *may* imply a lower quality of service with contracts, but this does not affect the average jail term.

Table 3.2 (continued)

Source	Comparison	Findings

21. Libraries:

| White (1983) | In-house libraries before and after federal aid. | After federal aid started in 1960s, productivity slowed as libraries added federally sponsored programs with lower marginal impact on output and fewer volunteers. Total factor productivity was at least 27% lower as a result. |

22. Liquor Stores:

| Simon and Simon (1987) | In-house versus private. | State stores have higher com-pensation rates, but higher sales per hour. If hours of op-eration (quality) are considered, private stores have lower costs. |

23. Military Support Services:

| Bennett and DiLorenzo (1983) | In-house versus private providers of equivalent services. | Average cost savings in base support services were 15%. |
| U.S. GAO (1985b) | Precontract bids versus postcontract costs for competitive Department of Defense contracts. | Most postcontract prices were in accord with bids. Some unsatisfactory performance seen in 33% of the con-tracts. Personnel turnover and low staffing were main problems. Contract price increases due largely to contract changes and Davis-Bacon wage regulations. |

Table 3.2 (continued)

Source	Comparison	Findings
U.S. GAO (1981a)	In-house versus contract.	Savings from both higher employee productivity and lower wages.
U.S. GAO (1985b)	Contract bids versus actual contract experience.	Contract costs increased over time in 95% of sample. In 89%, increases were too small to eliminate the net savings from contracting.[28] (Contracts were rebid in 35% of the cases due to failures of the initial contractor.) Main causes of the cost increases were general wage increases, rebidding of contracts, contract errors, or additional requirements not originally included.

24. Motor Vehicle Maintenance:

Campbell (1988)	In-house versus contract services.	Contractor costs are 1% to 38% below municipal costs for equivalent or higher levels of service. In conversions to contracting, wage levels generally remain similar, but the number of operating and overhead employees is reduced because of greater productivity.
Pomme- rehne and Schneider (1985)	In-house versus private costs in West Germany.	Private costs were 50% lower than public costs for automobile motor maintenance repairs.

Table 3.2 (continued)

Source	Comparison	Findings
Stolzenberg and Berry (1985)	Noncompetitive in-house versus competitive contract versus competitive in-house.	Competition resulted in lower costs through large reductions in personnel. Contracting saved approximately 17%. The lowest costs occurred where an in-house operator won competitive contracts. Costs averaged over 40% lower at these bases. Quality of maintenance was similar, but slightly better in government operations operating under competitive conditions. Higher government costs came from staffing for peak load demand, higher government fringe benefits and difficulties in hiring and firing.

25. Nursing Homes (health services) - also see Health Services (service category 13):

Lindsay (1975)	In-house (V.A.) versus contract.	Contract operated homes had 45% lower per day costs.

26. Parking:

Caponiti and Booher (1986)	In-house versus contract parking meter and parking restrictions enforcement.	Contracting is less costly, primarily because of lower fringe benefits and greater flexibility in meeting staffing requirements. Productivity (violations ticketed) improves as much as 10%, averaging 5%.

Table 3.2 (continued)

Source	Comparison	Findings

27. Parks and Recreation:

Stevens (1984)	In-house versus contract park turf maintenance.	Contract service had 28% lower costs and equivalent quality of service.
Savas (1987)	Government versus privately constructed sports facilities.	Costs of privately constructed sports arenas averaged 31% less that those of public arenas.
Holmes (1985)	In-house versus contract recreation program.	Former employees were able to offer municipality expanded program at 20% lower cost. Volunteers available to nonprofits reduce costs.
Poole (1980)	In-house versus private facilities operations and programs.	Cost savings of 20% obtained by privatizing. Savings come from more use of volunteers and better use of employees.
Fixler and Poole (1987), Valente and Manchester (1984)	In-house versus contracted profit and nonprofit organizations.	Contracting allowed maintenance of quality recreation services, even though budgets were reduced under California's Proposition 13 by as much as 50%.

28. Payroll and Data Processing (financial administration) - also see Assessment, Property Tax (service category 4):

Valente & Manchester (1984)	In-house versus private competitive contractors.	Contractor performed higher quality data processing service with cost savings of 15%.

Table 3.2 (continued)

Source	Comparison	Findings
Stevens (1984)	In-house versus private contractors.	No cost differences found after accounting for quality and other factors.

29. Police:

Deacon (1979)	In-house (local) versus intergovernmental.	Intergovernmental contracting saved 42%.
Mehay (1979)	In-house (local) versus contract with county (Lakewood Plan).	Contract costs were lower due to fewer police officers per capita. However, contract cities experienced higher rates of violent and property crimes. Net effects were probably negative for contract cities. Problem attributable to inability of contract cities to specify quality of service and monitor performance.
Mehay and Gonzalez (1985)	In-house monopoly versus in-house production with competition to serve additional jurisdictions.	Costs in counties that sell their police services to other jurisdictions are estimated to be 9% to 20% lower. The authors conclude that competition encourages police departments to keep their costs down.

30. Postal Service:

U.S. GAO (1982a)	In-house versus contracted routes.	Contracted delivery routes save up to 66% on delivery costs.

Table 3.2 (continued)

Source	Comparison	Findings
Hanke (1985a)	In-house versus contracted window service.	Contractors (retail stores with postal services) provided window service at 88% lower cost than USPS operated.
Savas (1987)	In-house versus private parcel delivery services.	Private firms have lower rates, faster delivery, lower losses from damage, better tracking systems, wider variety of services, and lower costs.

31. Printing:

Pomme-rehne and Schneider (1985)	In-house versus private in West Germany.	Private costs were 33% lower than public costs for commercial printing services.

32. Prisons:

Grant and Bast (1987)	In-house versus contract facilities and services.	Contractor prison construction costs are at least 45% lower than government averages. Service contracts for prison operations are at least 35% below average per/prisoner costs in recent cases.

33. Public Welfare:

Poole (1980)	In-house versus private variety of welfare services.	Privately supplied programs operating under competitive bidding saved 20% to over 60%.

Table 3.2 (continued)

Source	Comparison	Findings
Hatry (1983), Wedel, Katz, and Weick (1979)	In-house versus private contracting for vocational rehabilitation, childrens' protective services, and programs for the elderly.	Competitive contracting efforts have often devolved into single source contracting with little evidence of efficiency gains. Nonprofit firms are the predominate suppliers. Improved program characteristics are the primary objective of contracting, but no quantifiable quality information is available.

34. Railroads:

Bennett and DiLorenzo (1983)	In-house versus private providers of equivalent track repair. Article is based on GAO studies.	Private railroads repaired ties, replaced track, and surfaced rails at least 70% more efficiently.
Caves and Christensen (1980)	In-house (Canadian National) versus private (Canadian Pacific) costs and productivity differences.	No current productivity differences. The public firm substantially increased its efficiency after competition increased in 1965.

35. Refuse Collection (Sanitation other than Sewerage) - also see Street Cleaning (service category 41):

Collins and Downes (1977)	In-house versus private contracting-out in St. Louis area.	No significant cost differences. Private firms lost density economies because several firms served the same areas. Public suppliers had monopoly status.

Table 3.2 (continued)

Source	Comparison	Findings
Savas (1974, 1977a,b, 1980), Stevens and Savas (1978), Edwards and Ste- vens (1979)	In-house versus private monopoly franchise versus private nonfranchise firms.	Public supply was 40% to 60% more expensive than private. Private monopoly price was only slightly (5%) higher than price of private non-franchised collectors. Density economies offset otherwise higher costs.
Stevens (1984)	In-house versus competitive contract.	Cost savings of 22% were found, controlling for quality.
Hirsch (1965)	In-house (St. Louis City-County area) versus private firms.	No significant cost differences. Private competing suppliers lost density economies.
Kemper and Quigley (1976)	In-house versus private monopoly contract versus private nonfranchise versus municipal firms in Connecticut.	Municipal collection costs were 14% to 43% higher, but private nonfranchise costs were 25% to 36% higher than municipal collection. Loss of density economies increased costs of nonfranchise suppliers.
Kitchen (1976)	In-house versus private firms in forty-eight Canadian cities.	Municipal suppliers were more costly than proprietary firms.
Petrovic and Jaffee (1977)	In-house versus private contracting in midwestern cities.	Cost of city collection was 15% higher than the price of private contract collectors.

Table 3.2 (continued)

Source	Comparison	Findings
Pier, Vernon, and Wicks (1974)	In-house versus private firms in Montana.	Municipal suppliers appear to be more efficient, not controlling for quality and community characteristics. .
Savas (1977a)	In-house versus private firms in Minneapolis.	No significant cost differences if suppliers compete through tight control of municipal costs imposed by legislature using private costs as a comparison.
Savas (1981)	In-house and franchise contractors in a single district jurisdiction versus contractors and in-house in a multi-district setting.	The average number of bids per area increases when cities are divided into small districts. Competitive bidding leads to lower costs for contractor service. Cities that actively monitor municipal agencies using private contractor costs have lower average costs. No benefits are obtained without these policies.
Spann (1977)	In-house versus private firms. (Survey of literature.)	Public firms were 45% more costly.
36. Schools:		
Peterson (1981)	In-house versus private contractor- operated public schools.	Private contracting prompted small gains in math and reading and losses in other subjects. No cost savings.

Table 3.2 (continued)

Source	Comparison	Findings

37. Security Services (general maintenance of public buildings) - also see Cleaning Services (service category 7):

Hanke (1985a)	In-house versus private security guards.	Private security services save 50% or more.

38. Sewerage/ Waste Water Treatment:

Hanke (1985a)	In-house versus contractor built and operated treatment facilities.	Contractor costs average 20% to 50% less due to shorter construction lags and lower construction costs. Competition also reduces operating costs 20% to 50%.
Savas (1987), Moore (1988)	In-house versus outside contracts.	Contracted wastewater service is 20% to 50% less costly because federally financed projects involve higher construction (Davis-Bacon Act) and design costs.

39. Ship Repair and Maintenance:

Bennett and Johnson (1980)	In-house versus commercial tankers and oilers.	U.S. GAO reports that the private ship repair costs averaged 80% less than the U.S. Navy's costs.

40. Slaughterhouses:

Pausch (1976)	In-house versus private firms in 5 major West German cities.	Public firms were significantly more costly because of overcapacity and overstaffing.

Table 3.2 (continued)

Source	Comparison	Findings

---

41. Street Cleaning (refuse collection) - also see Refuse Collection (service category 35):

Stevens (1984)	In-house versus competitively contracted.	Contract cities have 43% lower costs after accoun-ting for quality and other factors.

42. Towing:

Kaiser (1976)	In-house versus contractors in N.Y.	Contract towing bids provided cost savings of more than 40%.

Transit: See Bus Service (service category 6).

Utilities: See Bus Service (service category 6), Electric Utilities (service category 10), and Water Utilities (service category 43).

43. Water Utilities (utilities) - also see Bus Services and Electric Utilities (service categories 6 and 10):

Crain and Zardkoohi (1978)	In-house versus private suppliers; comparisons of 112 firms and detailed case study of 2 firms that switched type of ownership.	Public firms were 40% less productive. Private firms had 25% lower costs. Public firms going private had 25% increase in output per employee. Private firm going public had an output per employee decrease of 40%.
Feigen-baum and Teeples (1982)	In-house versus private water companies.	No cost differences were found after controlling for other cost factors.

Table 3.2 (continued)

Source	Comparison	Findings
Mann and Mikesell (1976)	In-house versus private suppliers.	Found public modes were 20% more expensive after adjusting for input prices.
Morgan (1977)	In-house versus private suppliers covering 143 U.S. firms in six states.	Costs 15% higher for public firms.

44. Weather Forecasting:

Bennett and DiLorenzo (1983)	In-house versus private. Based on U.S. GAO studies.	Private weather forecasting contractors provided equivalent weather forecasting with 35% lower cost.

Sources: Borcherding, Pommerehne, and Schneider (1982), Domberger and Piggott (1986), and updates by the author.

Governmental contracting arrangements may occur between governments at the same level (e.g., mutual assistance agreements in fire fighting). At other times, a lower level of government has a choice between contracting for services from a higher level of government or producing the service in-house.

The best known form of competition between levels of government is the "Lakewood Plan," named after a community in California that opted to contract for various services from Los Angeles county agencies rather than produce these services in-house. Mixtures between self-provision and contract provision of a given service are also possible.[29]

Also included in the list in Table 3.2 are more that fifty studies critiqued by Borcherding, Pommerehne, and Schneider (1982). About a quarter of these earlier studies found, contrary to the others, that public agencies are equally or more efficient than contractors.[30] On the surface, these findings are inconsistent with the hypothesis that competition brings cost savings. On further examination, however, Borcherding discovered that, among the contrary studies judged to have used valid data and research methods, all involved government produced services that already compete with private providers.[31] Hence, no cost differences would necessarily be expected. Rather than contradicting the general findings of the other studies, these "exceptions" support the hypothesis that competition is critical to the efficient provision of government services.[32]

Finally, some reviewers of cost studies contend that the higher costs of in-house monopoly agencies are not due to inefficiency per se, but rather are due to conflicting and costly additional objectives that state and local in-house monopoly agencies are directed to pursue, or informally adopt.[33] Examples of imposition of such additional objectives include the dairy antisubstitution laws (discussed in chapter 1) and various in-state preference regulations that require purchasing from in-state vendors even if their prices are higher that competing out-of-state vendors.[34]

Although adopting noneconomic objectives may alter costs in some jurisdictions, detailed studies such as the Stevens study discussed above have reported systematic cost differences related to competition, community characteristics, and service levels. This evidence at least indicates that higher costs are not exclusively related to additional objectives imposed on in-house monopoly agencies.

Selection of Rate of Cost-Savings Estimates from Available Studies

The preceding subsections provided an overview of studies of cost savings from increased competition. This section discusses how the results of these studies can be organized to provide the rate of cost saving observations, s in equation (4), needed to calculate cost savings from increased competition. The principal task is matching rates of cost savings from the studies to expenditure categories available in the census data. This involves making several assumptions. The first assumption is that it is possible to make a reasonable concordance between the census categories and the studies. Ideally, services studied in cost savings studies would correspond directly to expenditure categories in the census. Indeed, in most cases there is a direct and obvious connection between budget categories available in the census and the services examined in studies of cost-savings rates contained in Table 3.2. In other cases, such direct matches are not possible. The best available technique for estimating cost savings in such cases is to group services into categories that broadly correspond to the census expenditure categories. As in other concordance efforts using economic data, the matching process generally assumes that a component service within a broader expenditure category is representative of the whole category. The matching process inevitably leads to contamination of the data and this could introduce an unknown bias in the estimates.[35] An effort is made in this study to minimize this potential bias by limiting the cost-savings estimates to categories in which the matches between the Census of Governments, International City Management Association, and research categories appear to be reasonably close.[36] Appendix E lists the census budget categories and the corresponding data sources and describes the degree of apparent agreement. A second assumption in the matching process is that jurisdictions provide services in ways that are sufficiently similar to make projections of cost savings transferable between jurisdictions.[37] Further, matching and using historical rates of cost savings assumes that cost savings realized in past cases may be replicated in future cases.[38]

Table 3.3 shows the estimates of the rate of cost savings gathered from empirical studies of individual government services listed in Table 3.2. The rates of cost savings on the left represent the lowest rates of total cost saving found in empirical studies of services in the expenditure category.[39] The higher rate of estimated cost savings on the right is generally taken from estimated cost-savings rates assembled by Clarkson and Fixler (1987).[40] These two sets of estimates for the rate of total cost savings (*s* in equation [4]) are used separately in the final cost-savings calculations to create upper and lower bound estimates for cost-savings.

EXTENT OF IN-HOUSE COMMERCIAL SERVICES: THE ICMA STUDY

Introduction

The second component needed to calculate cost savings is the current level of expenditures for commercial services that are produced on a monopoly in-house basis, E in equation (3). This is the expenditure base from which cost savings might be expected in future efforts to increase competition.[41]

Calculating E from equation (3) requires a combination of data on total current expenditures, the rates of total cost savings, and the proportion of jurisdictions that still use in-house monopoly production.

Data on government expenditures for different programs are available for state and local governments from the *Census of Governments*.[42] The rates of cost savings are presented in Table 3.3.[43]

The remaining information needed to calculate estimates of cost savings is the proportion of jurisdictions still utilizing in-house monopoly production in each service category.[44] A widely cited survey including this type of information was collected by the International City Managers Association in 1982. The results from the International City Managers Association's survey are used for the calculations here.

The International City Management Association Survey Data

Table 3.4 shows the organizational arrangements in the nearly 2,000 cities and counties that responded to the ICMA's survey.[45] In Table 3.4, the expenditure categories used in the ICMA's survey are grouped according to the corresponding census categories.

Table 3.3
Range of Rates of Cost Savings
in Local and State Activities

Expenditure Category [Table 3.2 Reference No(s)]	Base Estimated Percentage Cost Savings Rate[1]	Source of Base Estimate (from Table 3.2.)	High Estimated % Cost Savings: Clarkson & Fixler (1987) or others[2]
Airports [2]	25*	Moore (1987)	50*
Financial Administration [4,28]	0*	Stevens (1984)	35*
Fire Protection [11]	20	Poole (1976), Smith (1983)	65 Kristensen (1983), Hilke (1986)
General Maintenance of Public Buildings [7,37]	42*	Stevens (1984)	50*
Health Services [13,25]	0*	Schlesinger et al. (1986)	40*
Highways [14]	36*	Stevens (1984)	41*
Hospitals [15]	0*	Hatry (1983)	55*
Housing & Community Development [16]	20	Muth (1973), Rechnunghof Reinland-Pfalz (1972)	60 President's Comm. on Privatization (1988)

Table 3.3 (continued)

Expentiture Category [Table 3.2 Reference No(s)]	Base Estimated Percentage Cost Savings Rate[1]	Source of Base Estimate (from Table 3.2.)	High Estimated % Cost Savings: Clarkson & Fixler (1987) or others[2]
Libraries [21]	27*	White (1983)	35*
Parking Facilities [26]	5*	Caponiti & Booher (1986)	38*
Parks & Recreation [27]	28	Stevens (1984), Savas (1987)[3]	38
Public Welfare [33]	0*	Hatry (1983)	40*
Refuse Cllctn. [35,41]	22	Stevens (1984)	60 Savas (1974)[4]
Sewerage [38]	20	Moore (1988)	50 Moore (1988)
Transit [6]	10	Teal, Guiliano & Morlok (1986)[5]	65 Walters (1987)
Utilities [6,10,43]	0	Atkinson & Halvorsen (1986), Feigenbaum & Teeples (1982)	34

* Includes estimated cost savings in operating expenditures only. Capital outlays and cash assistance to individuals (public welfare payments) are excluded. See Appendix E for discussion.

NOTES:

[1]   The base cost-saving rate is generally the lowest estimate from an individual study except in those categories in which an estimate from the Stevens (1984) is available. The Stevens estimate, which control for quality or service and other factors, are used when they are available.

[2]   The high estimate is the high estimate from Clarkson and Fixler (1987) except where a specific study in Table 3.2 has a higher estimate. The reference(s) are given when the high cost savings estimate is not from Clarkson and Fixler.

[3]   Savas (1987) deals with construction costs rather than operating costs. He finds construction cost savings of 31% in private construction vs. public construction of sports facilities.

[4]   Also see other citations listed with Savas (1974) in Table 3.2.

[5]   The available studies cover bus services. Other transit systems are included on the assumption that savings would be similar. The savings rates used here are conservative estimates of the percentage savings to government.
    The savings rates used here are savings rates for all operating expenditures. See Table 3.2, service category 6. Government expenditures, however, are only a portion of total operating expenses because some costs are paid through fare collections. As a result, for example, if a government initially subsidizes 50% of costs, savings in operating costs of 10% will result in a 20% reduction in government subsidies (assuming fare collections remain the same).
    See Appendix E for more discussion.

Table 3.4
Service Delivery Approaches of the ICMA Survey Respondents, Arranged by Corresponding Census and ICMA Expenditure Categories (% Taking a Particular Approach, of Jurisdictions Reporting at Least Some Expenditures in the Category*)

Service Category Census / ICMA Survey	% In-House Only	% Inter-Govern.	% with For-Prof. Contract+	% with Non-Profit	% with Vol.
Airports					
Airport Operation	39	26	33	4	1
Financial Administration					
Payroll	86	3	10	1	0
Tax Bill Process.	65	9	11	6	0
Tax Assessing	57	29	7	4	0
Delinquent Tax Collection	62	20	10	3	0
Average	67.5				
Fire Protection					
Fire Prevention and Suppression	69	9	1	3	18
General Maintenance of Public Buildings					
Bldng./Grnds. Maintenance	73	4	20	1	1
Building Security	86	3	8	1	0
Average	79.5				
Health Services					
Public Health Programs	26	30	9	27	8

Table 3.4 (continued)

Service Category Census / ICMA Survey	% In-House Only	% Inter-Govern.	% with For-Prof. Contract+	% with Non-Profit	% with Vol.
Highways					
Street Repair	65	5	27	1	0
Snow Plowing	79	4	14	0	0
Traffic Signals	54	14	27	2	0
Street Light Op.	30	21	53	2	0
Average	57.0				
Hospitals					
Hospital Op.	18	25	31	27	2
Housing & Community Development					
Publ./Elderly Housing	21	43	13	18	1
Libraries					
Library Op.	50	28	1	10	12
Parking Facilities					
Parking Lot/ Garage	75	7	14	2	0
Parking Meters	88	4	7	0	0
Average	81.5				

Table 3.4 (continued)

Service Category Census / ICMA Survey	% In-House Only	% Inter-Govern.	% with For-Prof. Contract+	% with Non-Profit	% with Vol.
Parks & Recreation					
Recreation Serv.	52	9	6	13	20
Rec. Fac. Oper. & Maintenance	58	9	17	9	10
Parks Landscaping	76	5	10	2	4
Op. of Convention Center	70	10	8	6	2
Op. of Cult. Arts	11	11	9	39	32
Op. of Museums	21	16	5	32	21
Average	48.0				
Public Welfare					
Child Welfare	27	28	6	24	6
Refuse Collection (Sanitation other than Sewerage)					
Residential Ref.	49	8	50	0	0
Commercial Ref.	29	7	63	0	0
Solid Waste Disposal	38	31	33	2	0
Street Cleaning	84	3	9	0	0
Average	50.0				

Table 3.4 (continued)

Service Category Census / ICMA Survey	% In-House Only	% Inter-Govern.	% with For-Prof. Contract+	% with Non-Profit	% with Vol.
Sewerage Treatment					
Utility Meter Reading	64	9	20	1	0
Utility Billing	62	10	22	1	0
Average	63.0				
Transit					
Bus System Op.	26	42	29	9	1
Paratransit Op.	19	29	27	21	8
Average	22.5				
Utilities					
Utility Meter Reading	64	9	20	1	0
Utility Billing	62	10	22	1	0
Bus System Op.	26	42	29	9	1
Paratransit Op.	19	29	27	21	8
Average	42.8				

* Total % may be more or less than 100% because some supply approaches are not listed and some jurisdictions may use more than one approach.
+ Includes franchises.

The percentage of jurisdictions exclusively utilizing in-house monopoly production is shown in the first column to the right of the listing of expenditure categories. The other columns show percentages of jurisdictions using other production arrangements that involve increased competition. Percentages may add to more than 100% since some jurisdictions use more than one of the methods of increasing competition.

Inspection of the statistics in Table 3.4 reveals that services are produced in many different ways in different jurisdictions. The table shows that a few services, such as parking meter maintenance and building security, are primarily financed at only one level of government. Many services, however, are financed at both the city and county levels of government. Some additional services such as public and elderly housing, hospitals, and libraries evidence high levels of intergovernmental funding and operation.   Differences also appear in the production of services. Some services, such as street repairs, code inspections, and payroll operations are almost exclusively produced in-house (and always have been), whereas others, such as paratransit services, recreation programs, and fire protection, are commonly produced by for-profit contractors, nonprofit groups, or volunteers.[46] For-profit contractors provide services in a plurality of jurisdictions in commercial waste collection, street light operations, and operation and management of hospitals.

Data from the "% In-House Only" column in Table 3.4 are used to produce the m variable in equation (4); whereas m is the proportion of jurisdictions that continue to use monopoly in-house production. When there is only one ICMA expenditure category associated with a census expenditure category, the value of m is determined directly from the listing in Table 3.4. When more than one ICMA category is included in a census category, the average of the ICMA categories is used for m. This average is shown at the bottom of the listing of ICMA categories under each census category.   For example, the census category of Financial Administration encompasses four ICMA categories: Payroll Processing, Tax Bill Processing, Tax Assessing, and Delinquent Tax Collection.   The estimate of m for the entire Financial Administration category is the average "% In-House Only" for these four categories, 67.5% in this case.

POTENTIAL TOTAL COST SAVINGS CALCULATIONS

The estimates of cost savings from increased competition are calculated using equation (4): $S = smT / (1 - s + ms)$. As described previously, s is the rate of cost savings taken from studies of the effects of increased competition on costs of government financed services (Table 3.3).

Two levels of savings rates are used. One is an upper bound and the other is a lower bound estimate. The value m is the proportion of jurisdictions continuing to provide a service as an in-house monopoly (Table 3.4) and T is total expenditures for a service taken from the *Census of Governments* shown in Table 3.5. Table 3.5 also shows total estimated expenditures in the jurisdictions with in-house monopoly production.

The annual potential total cost savings for each expenditure category are shown in Table 3.6.[47]

The base estimate of cost savings from increased competition summed across expenditure categories is $14.0 billion and the high estimate is $55.1 billion, annually.[48] The estimated present value of a perpetual stream of cost savings of this magnitude is $155.1 billion to $612.7 billion.[49]

Table 3.5
Total and In-House Monopoly Expenditures
(billions of 1986-1987 dollars)

Service	Total Expenditures "T"	Base Estimate "E"	High Estim. "E"
Airports	2.495	1.148	1.148
Financial Administ.	13.438	9.071	10.235
Fire Protection	11.927	8.774	10.306

Table 3.5 (continued)

Service	Total Expenditures "T"	Base Estimate "E"	High Estim. "E"
General Maint. of Public Bldngs.	3.248	2.825	2.877
Health Serv.	17.970	4.672	6.637
Highways	26.333	17.759	18.034
Hospitals	41.338	7.441	11.034
Housing and Comm. Dev.	12.591	3.140	5.027
Libraries	3.171	1.833	1.922
Parking Facilities	.510	.420	.431
Parks and Recreation	11.792	6.625	6.876
Public Welfare	66.169	17.866	25.234
Refuse Coll.	7.002	3.934	5.001
Sewerage	15.618	10.626	12.073
Transit Subs.	.268	.071	.122
Utilities	69.692	29.828	34.347
Total	304.6	126.0	151.8

Table 3.6
Estimated Annual Total Potential Cost Savings in
Different Services Accumulated Nationwide -
Combined State and Local Expenditures
(billions of 1986-1987 dollars)

Service	Base Estimate	High Estimate
Airports	0.287	0.287
Financial Administration	0.0	3.582
Fire Protection	0.737	2.814
General Maintenance of Public Buildings	1.187	1.439
Health Services	0.0	2.655
Highways	6.393	7.033
Hospitals	0.0	4.942
Housing and Community Development	0.628	3.016
Libraries	0.376	0.511
Parking Facilities	0.021	0.082
Parks and Recreation	1.326	1.672
Public Welfare	0.0	10.094
Refuse Collection	0.865	3.001
Sewerage	2.125	6.036

Table 3.6 (continued)

Service	Base Estimate	High Estimate
Transit Subsidies	0.014	0.079
Utilities	0.0	7.900
Total	14.0	55.1

NOTES

1. Local governments include counties, municipalities (cities, towns, villages, etc.), school districts, and special districts.

2. U.S. Council of Economic Advisors (1988, pp. 283, 343, 344). More than $150 billion in capital expenditures were also undertaken by state and local governments.

3. The judiciary system and the legislative system are primarily involved in policy formulation. Police functions are considered to be inherently governmental because they so frequently deal with use of force by the government and with issues of personal freedom that are uniquely governmental responsibilities.

4. Several cities, including Phoenix, Arizona, began considering contractingout because of the decline in funding available from Civilian Employment Training Act (CETA) grants. See Gordon (1984) and Valente and Manchester (1984, p. 170).

5. Nonprofit firms and volunteers have widely been used to provide various types of social services. In the ICMA survey (Valente and Manchester, 1984, p. xv), for example, nonprofit firms provided paratransit services in 21% of jurisdictions and volunteers provides the services in 8%. In fire suppresision, the figures were 3% and 18% respectively. For additional perspectives on the use of volunteers in local government, see Weisbrod (1977), Rose-Ackerman (1986), Valentine and Manchester (1984, pp. 244-70), and McChesney (1986).

6. Expenditure levels for individual categories listed in the *Census of Governments* were adjusted to include pension payments. The pension

category expenditures in the census were distributed in proportion to total nonpension expenditures in the other census expenditure categories.

7. In contrast, data used to calculate expenditure levels for the Federal government were based on occupational classifications. As in chapter 2, the estimated cost savings calculated in this chapter do not include government budget reductions from privatization through complete service shedding.

8. Additional information on competition in education may become available in the near future as private contracts to provide public education become more common and as school systems experiment with systems that allow parents a choice of schools. See, for example, Putka (1991) and Bacon (1990).

9. A separate set of estimates does include cost-savings estimates for several of these categories based on cost-savings rates proposed by Clarkson and Fixler (1987).

10. The calculation of the potential total cost savings in jurisdictions with in-house monopolies is illustrated in the following example. Assume that total refuse collection expenditures from the census are T = $200 million, that in-house monopoly jurisdictions account for m = 70% of all jurisdictions, and that the rate of potential total cost savings in jurisdictions with increased competition is s = 25%. Equation (4) shows potential total cost savings from future increases in competition as $S = smT / (1 - s + ms)$ = 0.25 x 0.7 x $200 / [1 - .25 + (0.7 x 0.25)] = $37.8 million.

11. The same limitations and cautions concerning application of past total cost-savings rates to future projects discussed in chapter 2 apply here as well.

12. Because consumers are concerned about both price and quality of services, they will not always favor a decline in costs if it results in a decline in quality. Therefore, it is potentially important to control for service quality in evaluating cost-savings effects. Otherwise, reduced costs from reduced quality may be inappropriately treated in the same manner as reduced costs from improved efficiency or lower economic rents.

13. Stevens (1984).

14. See Table 4.1 in particular.

15. Los Angeles area communities were used because the proportion of cities with experience in competitive contracting is relatively high there.

16. Pooling means using observations from all the services together to examine relationships that apply across services.

17. In this analysis, cities with in-house monopoly agencies and cities using competitive contractual arrangements are paired on the basis of similar characteristics. Comparisons using matched pair samples are conducted by using nonparametric statistics.

18. The cost comparisons in Stevens (1984) assume that institutional arrangements have been in place long enough so that management has had an opportunity to adjust the capital stock to be as cost efficient as possible. The Los Angeles area where the data were collected has a long history of contracting for various services (see Mehay, 1979). The sample of cities with contracting was originally generated from surveys conducted one to several years before the cost data were collected by Stevens (see Stevens, 1984, pp. 10-20). If rates of cost savings are measured before full adjustments have been made, the short-run savings rate observed are likely to understate the long-run rates and bias the total potential cost-savings estimates downward.

19. Comparisons of median values of costs among sampled cities are generally consistent with the average cost comparisons. In only one cost/efficiency measure out of twenty, cost per cubic yard of debris in street cleaning, does the comparison of means differ in direction from the comparison of median values. In this one efficiency comparison, the mean for contract cities is 14% lower than the mean for cities with in-house monopoly agencies, whereas the median for cities with in-house monopolies is 3% lower than the median for cities using competitive contracting. This occurred because two cities with in-house monopoly agencies had much higher street cleaning costs than any other cities of either type.

In quality measures, mean and median comparisons differ in direction in five cases out of seventeen. Two of these relate to payroll operations where no mean cost differences were found. Two others involve percentage changes of less than 2%. In the final example, comparison of mean values showed that the quality of trash collection services in cities with in-house monopoly agencies is rated 10% better than trash collection in cities using competitive contracting, whereas the comparison of median values shows that quality in cities with competitive contracting is rated 25% better than quality in cities with in-house monopoly agencies. The difference in the comparisons is due to bifurcated observations for the cities using competitive contracting with most of these cities having very high quality, but a few having low quality ratings.

20. Additional examination of the cost and service quality data show, as might be expected, that the distributions of average costs and quality for cities with competitive contracting and cities with in-house monopoly agencies overlap to some degree in all of the services studied. (That is,

the highest cost city with competitive contracts has higher costs than the lowest cost city with in-house monopoly agencies.) However, the cost and quality distributions often are not symmetrical around the mean. The distributions for cities with in-house monopoly agencies contain extremely high cost values more frequently than the distributions for cities with competitive contracting.

21. Stevens (1984, pp. 523-530).

22. Borcherding, Pommerehne, and Schneider (1982).

A general review of Canadian experience with privatization is contained in Walker (1988).

23. For a critical analysis of the few systematic empirical studies with contrary conclusions (summarized by Millwood, 1982), see Bennett and Johnson (1981, pp. 43-47) and Borcherding, Pommerehne, and Schneider (1982). For examples of particularly unsuccessful privatization efforts, see Bailey (1987), and AFSCME (1983, 1988).

24. This internal audit of the reasonableness of bids helps to avoid litigation by private contractors who lose in a bid and might otherwise claim that the in-house bid was unrealistically low. Separate reviews by the city's attorney and finance

25. Hatry (1983) reported that city agencies in Phoenix had submitted low bids in ten of twenty-two cases up to 1982. For example, city workers won back Phoenix's large contract for refuse collection starting in 1984 (see Moore, 1987, p. 64).

26. Savas (1981).

27. This review does not include references to cost savings estimates in Clarkson & Fixler (1987) since his estimates result from his synopsis of the literature rather than from additional empirical work.

28. This comparison overstates the effect of cost increases on rates of cost savings. This study compared contract costs months or years after the contract was first let with in-house costs at the time the contract was first let. It ignores the fact that cost for the whole economy increased over time. Therefore, part of the cost increase in the contract is due to this economy-wide phenomenon and similar increases in government costs would likely have occurred as well.

29. For example, several Maryland communities provide their own police patrols during part of the day and contract with the county government for police services at other times. The community receives a rebate on county taxes for the services that it provides itself.

30. Domberger and Piggott (1986).

The contradictory studies include Meyer (1975); Spann (1977); Lindsay (1976); Finsinger (1981); Caves and Christensen (1980); Collins and Downes (1977); Hirsch (1965); Savas (1977a); and Pier, Vernon, and Wicks (1974).

Wolf (1988, p. 138) reports some additional findings showing higher costs in private utility firms. He finds that the higher costs in these studies include distortions induced by economic regulation of private firms and higher marketing costs in private firms that sell directly to consumers rather than selling primarily at the wholesale level, as a larger proportion of government utilities do. Both of these are largely exogenous cost factors that should be controlled for in assessing relative efficiency.

31. In some services studied, competition came from private firms producing a substitute service rather than from private firms competing to produce for the government. In others, private firms competed with government bureaus to produce for the government.

Similar results have been found recently for school bus transportation services. Wolf (1988, p. 139).

32. Milward (1982) also found several studies to contradict the cost savings through privatization hypothesis. He did not consider whether increased competition accompanied the privatization.

33. Millward (1982), Starr (1987), and Wolf (1988, p. 139).

34. Pelkmans (1988).

35. If the cost structures for various services contained within the same broad census expenditure category are quite different, cost-savings estimates derived from studies of one component service may not provide an accurate estimate for cost savings for another service, even if it is in the same category.

36. See Appendix E for more detailed description of the matches between expenditure categories used in the three primary data sources.

37. Given the widespread, indeed worldwide, research findings of cost reductions through increased competition in government provided commercial services, this assumption seems reasonable.

38. There is no dispositive evidence on this question, however, continued findings of 20% to 50% cost savings are inconsistent with any rapid decline in the rate of cost savings over time. The theory of public choice yields mixed hypotheses. On one hand, larger opportunities for cost savings might be expected to be identified first, since larger opportunities are likely to be more obvious, and therefore cost-savings rates might be expected to decline over time as the stock of dramatic savings opportunities is exhausted. In contrast, if larger savings are likely to disturb the interests of more people, the political difficulties of providing large cost savings might have limited past cost-savings efforts to less dramatic cost-savings opportunities.

39. The studies reviewed and judged to be "reliable" by Borcherding were included for consideration.   Those Borcherding judged to be unreliable were excluded.

40. In some cases, other studies found higher cost savings rates than Clarkson and Fixler. When this occurs, the higher rate is used.

In Clarkson and Fixler (1987), the upper bound rate of cost savings figures were reduced by half when applied to government enterprises (as opposed to in-house government agencies.)

41. We assume that all potential cost savings have already occurred where some institution for increasing competition has been introduced in the jurisdiction for a particular service. To the extent that additional total cost savings might be realized by providing additional competition in these jurisdictions, we underestimate potential total cost savings in the calculation here.

We also assume that additional reductions in costs from increased competition are possible in jurisdictions that provide services through in-house monopolies.   This assumption could overstate the degree of potential cost savings if in-house production persists because it has successfully competed against other potential suppliers.   Systematic, periodic competition between in-house and outside suppliers, which is likely to minimize in-house production costs, is still quite rare, however, in state and local governments. This assumption could also overstate the degree of potential cost savings if interagency or interjurisdictional competition have been so effective that they preclude further cost savings in remaining in-house monopoly situations. In defense of the assumption that this is not the case, it can be observed that many of the studies reviewed for Table 3.3 involved situations in which interagency or interjurisdictional competition could have been present.   Nonetheless, significant rates of cost savings from increased competition were found. Consequently, the cost savings observed in the empirical studies and the potential total cost savings being considered in this report, both may be incremental competition effects rather than absolute competition effects, which may be larger. In both instances, an upward bias in the cost-savings estimates seems unlikely to be material.

42. The original and modified total expenditure figures are displayed in Table 3.5.

43. The total expenditure figure for each expenditure category includes operating expenditures, capital expenditures, direct transfers to individuals, and an allocation of retirement and other trust funds. The trust fund expenditures are allocated in proportion to operating expenditures in the category. For example, financial administration accounted for 2.22% of total current expenditures in state and local

governments ($12.2 billion/$550.1 billion), therefore, expenditures for this category include 2.22% of trust fund expenditures (0.0222 x $50.82 billion = $1.13 billion).

44. U.S. Department of Commerce (1987).

45. Appendix D contains some additional updated information about levels of privatization in different services taken from a more recent study of Florida local governments.

46. Although utilizing volunteers represents an important method of reducing government expenditures for some types of services, some communities may not be able to attract volunteers and so savings from the use of volunteers might not be available to them. To avoid assuming that volunteers are universally available, the cost-savings estimates have been reduced for services in which the volunteer category in the ICMA data exceeds 10%. When this criteria is met, the cost-savings estimates are reduced by the ratio of the ICMA volunteer figure divided by the proportion of that service that is not categorized as "exclusive" in-house production. Cost-savings estimates are reduced by 58% for fire fighting, 24% for libraries, and 28.5% of parks and recreation on this basis.

47. An alternative set of estimates of potential total cost savings from increased competition appears in Clarkson's and Fixler's study *The Role of Privatization in Florida's Growth* (Clarkson and Fixler, 1987, Chapter IV). The Florida study uses information from the Stevens study and other studies to estimate cost savings for a wide variety of state and local government services in Florida. The study finds annual total potential cost savings, state-wide, of $1.038 billion to $1.894 billion, in 1986 dollars. If it is assumed that the level and distribution of government services in Florida is similar to that in the rest of the country on an average per capita basis, the estimated total cost savings from privatization of commercial government output on a nationwide basis would total $24.1 to $44.0 billion annually. This stream of savings has a present value of $268 to $489 billion, based on a discount rate of 9%.

A similar study has been made of budgets for jurisdictions in the state of Illinois (King, 1986). This study included an examination of potential areas of cost savings through increased competition (largely by contracting out). The study identified potential total cost savings from contracting out of 10.2% for city government, 40.4% for county government, and 10.6% for state government. The Illinois study specifically excluded public safety and judicial expenditures, except vehicle maintenance operations for these functions, as well as special districts and municipally operated utilities. If national projections are made from the Illinois study, potential total cost savings would be $40.7

billion annually.   The present value would be $452 billion using a 9% interest rate.

48. These cost savings figures are 6.8% and 18.2%, respectively, of total expenditures in the expenditure categories included. The figures are 2.7% and 7.1%, respectively, of total expenditures by state and local governments in all expenditure categories.

49. Based on a 9% discount rate.

4

Sources of Cost Savings

INTRODUCTION

As noted in chapter 1, total cost savings associated with increased competition might result both in reduced wages and in real resource cost savings.[1] Some commentators have been concerned that increased competition results primarily or exclusively in reduced wages rather than real resource cost savings.[2]

If wages are initially above the competitive level, reducing wage levels may benefit consumers by improving efficiency.[3] Excessive wage rates may lead to distortions in economic choices in the same way that prices above competitive levels in other inputs do.[4] That is, they may result in insufficient production of some goods and excessive production of other goods, with a net loss of consumer welfare. On the other hand, if wages are initially at the competitive level, reducing wage levels may be detrimental to consumers. Such reductions in wages to levels below the competitive level would occur only if increasing competition leads to monopsony power.[5]

Although it is theoretically possible that shifting from in-house government production to private contracting or other forms of increased competition could lead to monopsony power, this seems quite unlikely.[6] Aside from competing with each other for qualified workers, contractors and competing government agencies also must compete with private industry for workers with similar job skills. Hence, qualified workers are likely to have a wide array of potential employers to choose from, and any contractor or government agency that offers less than competitive wage rates should shortly find it difficult to attract and retain qualified employees.

Savings in real resources are generally viewed as economically beneficial to consumers because the resources released by greater efficiency can be utilized to produce more of other goods and services that consumers desire.   However, some forms of productivity gains may involve exploiting or underpaying workers or other inputs in the production process, rather than improving management. In that case, output per worker may be high due to changes (in work rules, for example) that result in paying workers less than a competitive return on their investments in job specific expertise and training.[7]

Two factors tend to mitigate this potential concern about exploitation of workers. First, most government jobs subject to increased competition from outside producers (or other government agencies) do not involve highly specialized skills that are likely to be unique to one particular government job. Indeed, the concept of emphasizing competition in commercial services produced by the government is based on the comparability of job skills in the private and public sectors. As long as workers have transferable skills, the ability of an employer to engage in economic hold-up of workers is strictly limited by the workers' ability to quit and obtain comparable work elsewhere. Since this appears to be the predominant case in the jobs being considered for increased competition, the concern about economic exploitation of workers should be negligible. Second, there is little reason to believe that contractors or other government agencies that might increase competition have substantial market power that could make it difficult for workers to switch employers if these employers tried to pay less than competitive wages.

The theoretical distinction between sources of cost savings has been addressed in several empirical studies, although less frequently than the total cost savings question. The predominant conclusion from these empirical analyses is that a substantial portion of total cost savings result directly in real resource savings (i.e., less inputs to obtain the same output). Chapter 4 present additional material in this regard. The magnitudes of the real resources expended to capture economic rents remains unknown.

STUDIES OF SOURCES OF FEDERAL GOVERNMENT COST SAVINGS

Detailed analyses of cost reductions resulting from A-76 studies (federal government studies of the feasibility of contracting with private firms to provide services previously produced by government employees) indicate a variety of sources of cost savings. They represent reductions in real resources used in producing the services as well as reductions in the wages paid to employees performing the service. Available information generally *is consistent* with the hypothesis that contracting for commercial services often provides substantial savings in real resources by increasing labor and other types of productivity.[8] Evidence also suggests that a substantial portion of savings from reorganizing *in-house* production (prompted by competition from outside suppliers) comes from increased productivity.

Some direct evidence on sources of reduced costs is available from detailed studies conducted by the U.S. General Accounting Office (GAO).[9] In an August 1981 study of cleaning costs, for example, GAO found that the General Services Administration's (GSA) cleaning costs at the time were, on average, 50% higher than the costs of contracting for similar services from private firms.[10] Differences between GSA's costs and those of private cleaning firms serving comparable commercial buildings were even greater. In investigating the causes of such large cost differences, GAO found that although GSA's higher wage levels were in part responsible for its higher costs, productivity differences were also a very important cause.[11] In one area of the country, for example, there was no starting wage differential, yet cost differences of approximately 25% were still present. Further investigation revealed that a substantial portion of the difference in costs was attributable to differences in productivity. GSA employees cleaned an average of 9.8% less area per hour than contractors' employees and 17% less than employees of private cleaning firms working for landlords.[12] No apparent differences in the quality of cleaning were reported. In one region, the productivity difference between GSA staff and landlords' staffs averaged 30%. In the region with no wage differential, the productivity difference was 10%, but this difference was smaller than in other areas, in part, because labor agreements in that region required some overstaffing in private buildings covered by union contracts.[13] Researchers attributed the productivity advantages of private operations to management expectations of workers, good supervision, use of modern equipment, employee motivation, innovative work techniques and procedures, and off-hours scheduling of cleaning services.[14]

Other GAO studies of Defense Department contracting of commercial services have also concluded that *both* wage rates and productivity differences are major reasons why contractors have lower costs. Again, the wage differences reported by GAO were attributed to problems in calculating required wages under the Davis Bacon Act.[15] GAO found that the government's system of gathering information on wage rates for comparable work was faulty.[16]

More recently, Rand Corporation researchers also investigated sources of cost savings in A-76 studies. Examining vehicle maintenance operations at U.S. domestic military air bases, the Rand investigators found that time series "data suggest that A-76 leads to a drastic reduction in labor requirements with no apparent increase in the use of labor-saving capital equipment. These labor productivity increases appear to be the major cause of savings associated with A-76 procedures."[17] Further, increased labor productivity was associated with both in-house and contract operations following A-76 reviews. Cross-sectional data show that both in-house and contract costs following A-76 studies were lower than traditional in-house operations, again primarily because of lower labor requirements.

The Rand researchers observed no systematic *wage* differentials between contract and in-house programs. This may be attributable to the limited number of personnel who have training in maintaining specialized air force vehicles. The Rand team observed that the vehicle maintenance work force was quite stable even when contractors changed.[18] However, government *benefits* packages were found to be more generous than those of private employers. This was particularly true for veterans whose military service gave them advanced seniority in qualifying for annual leave. The higher level of benefits for in-house workers explained much of the reason that in-house bids usually lost to contract bids even though in-house bids (after reorganizations) often proposed similar productivity increases.[19]

Empirical findings on in-house reorganizations under A-76 point to substantial productivity improvements associated with A-76 reviews generally. The techniques commonly cited for reducing costs of internal production through management reviews include the following: consolidation of functions to realize economies of scale or scope in equipment and supervision, obtaining updated equipment and utilizing improved production techniques, reorganizing the structure of production and rationalizing operating procedures, increasing use of incentive pay systems where possible, and reevaluating the grades of positions to utilize the lowest grade personnel capable of doing the job.[20] If internal management reorganization can provide cost savings of 20% without any changes in wage scales, and if private contractors can utilize the same types of organizational changes to reduce costs, then it is reasonable to conclude that part of the savings from contracting represents organizational efficiencies. As discussed in chapter 1, during the process of conducting in-house evaluations and reorganizations, bids from private contractors provide two vital ingredients, a yardstick against which to measure in-house costs and real incentives for management and workers to cooperate in assessing potential cost savings. In-house evaluations and reorganizations without the benefit of outside competition may be less successful.[21]

STUDIES OF SOURCES OF LOCAL AND STATE GOVERNMENT COST SAVINGS

Evidence about the relative extent of productivity improvements and reduced wage premiums that stem from increased competition at the local level is available primarily in the 1984 Housing and Urban Development Department study (Stevens, 1984). The HUD researchers found that differences in costs between cities are significantly related to more efficient management practices, independent of whether the city contracts or produces services in-house.[22] However, cities that contract were more likely to use efficient management practices. Cities with low costs (either contract or in-house) tended to require that managers be responsible for availability of personnel and serviceability of equipment. Integrated responsibility apparently reduced the tendency to "pass the buck" when support services or equipment are not delivered in a timely, efficient manner, or when sufficient work crews were not available. Cities with high costs tended to release managers from many direct personnel supervision responsibilities such as hiring, firing, and assessing penalties for tardiness, thus making the managers less accountable for performance.

Cities providing a service through in-house production were more likely to fall into the high cost, less-accountability group of cities because the use of more formal and elaborate personnel procedures carried over from their inherently governmental functions. Such formalized personnel procedures may be efficient in the context of inherently governmental services even if they reduce productivity in producing commercial services.[23]

Cities with in-house agencies also tended to utilize a government-wide central equipment maintenance system with its own set of government managers. This may have further weakened accountability of the managers of individual government service agencies by removing equipment readiness from their control.[24] In this regard, the HUD authors concluded that cost savings from economies of scale in the communities studied were less important in restraining costs than in delineating clear lines of authority and responsibility.

The few cities with in-house production that organized themselves to preserve management lines of responsibility were better able to provide equivalent services at costs much closer to those of contract cities. However, it appears that the incentives or ability to maintain clear lines of management responsibility were attenuated in most cities that lacked the competitive environment provided by contracting.

When contractors were compared to in-house agencies (not subject to competition) across services, it was found that contractors were more likely to use longer shifts[25] and grant less vacation, use part-time and minimally qualified employees for any particular job, use fewer formal procedures, use somewhat less labor-intensive techniques, and grant line supervisors both more responsibility for a whole service and more power in supervising personnel.[26] Wages of contract workers were found to be somewhat lower than those of in-house workers in most services.[27] An exception was asphalt overlay, where contract employee wages were 58% higher than in-house worker's wages.[28] Among services other than asphalt overlay, wages of contract employees were on average 13.9% lower. The average of the percentage differences in wages for all services was less than 5%. Fringe benefits of in-house workers were also higher than those for contract workers, again with the exception of asphalt overlay.

Table 4.1 shows how differences in total compensation rates (wages and fringe benefits) affected the cost reduction results from the HUD study. By subtracting out the effects of compensation differences, estimates of real resource savings from increasing competition can be obtained. Taking traffic signals maintenance as an example, column 1 shows that average total cost in contract cities was 64.1% of that in in-house agency cities. As shown in column 2, labor costs for traffic signals maintenance accounted for 54% of total costs in contract cities. Column 3 displays the difference in compensation rates between contract cities and cities with in-house production. In this case, in-house cities paid 23.33% higher average compensation for traffic signals maintenance. If contract cities paid as much as in-house cities, their costs would have been higher. When contract cities' costs are adjusted to take account of these wage and benefit differences, it is found that their costs for traffic signal maintenance are 72.2% of total in-house cities' costs (column 4). This means that after accounting for differences in compensation, costs for traffic signal maintenance in contract cities were on average 27.8% lower than those in cities with in-house production (column 5). As described above, without this adjustment, the contract cities' costs were 35.9% (100% - 64.1%) lower than those in the in-house cities.[29]

Column 5 in Table 4.1 indicates that removing the difference in rates of compensation narrows, but does not generally eliminate, the total cost differences. In the case of payroll processing, the adjustment leads to a cost increase.

In all of the other services, cost savings would still be realized even if no compensation differences existed. These cost savings are real resource savings.

Table 4.1
Cost Savings Unrelated to Wage and Benefit Rates

(1)	(2)	(3)	(4)	(5)
Initial Index of Relative Costs	Labor Cost as a % of Total Costs in Contract Cities	Relative Labor Costs in Municipal and Contract Cities*	Index of Relat. Costs Removing Differences Due to Wages and Benefits	% Cost Savings Not from Lower Wages or Benefits
Street Cleaning				
69.9	44	35.56	80.8	19.2
Janitorial Services				
57.8	56	69.79	80.4	19.6
Trash Collection				
78.1	39	32.19	87.9	12.1
70.4	39	32.19	79.2	20.9
Payroll Processing				
100.0	49	15.89	107.8	-7.8
Traffic Signals				
64.1	54	23.33	72.2	27.8
Asphalt Overlay				
51.0	30	-37.79	45.2	54.8
Turf Maintenance				
71.4	71	52.39	98.0	2.0
Street Trees				
73.0	70	29.40	88.0	12.0

Source: Stevens (1984, pp. 541-543).

* Calculated as (Labor Costs in Municipal Cities / Labor Costs in Contract Cities) - 1.

Cost savings from compensation differences averaged 11.53% per service, whereas total cost differences averaged 29.4%. Cost reductions averaging 17.83% would have still been realized even if compensation rates had been identical. The proportion of cost savings attributable to compensation differences was by far the largest in turf maintenance, where they accounted for 93% of total cost savings. On average, compensation accounted for slightly less than 40% (39.2%) of total cost savings. Over 60% of cost savings were not attributable to differences between the rates of compensation.

It should be noted that this table overstates the expected change in total costs of imposing a regulation that contractors pay the same level of wages as municipalities. Calculations for this table assume that the contractors would retain the same number of laborers, utilize them the same way, and employ the same organization and technology. In fact, contractors might well be expected to adjust to such a requirement by using less labor, using labor differently, and/or utilizing different organizational forms and technologies. Results using two alternative methods of treating overhead are shown for refuse collection. Both estimates are consistent with the results for the other services.

This analysis provides strong evidence that, although cost savings from increased competition may involve reduced wage premiums, an equal or larger portion comes from increased productivity.

CONCLUSION

To summarize the cost savings discussion, economic theory and available studies at the federal and local/state levels indicate that both outside contracting and in-house reorganization (prompted by competition from outside suppliers) can substantially reduce the costs of government financed commercial services, including real resource savings.

Portions of the cost reductions observed in this research have involved productivity improvements that save real resources and portions have involved wage or benefit reductions.[30] Productivity increases because competition from outside suppliers, either directly or indirectly, increases incentives to innovate and attend to productivity issues. Society would obtain real cost savings from increased competition, even if the compensation effects were eliminated.

The compensation reductions occurred primarily because many government workers, for statutory or other reasons, receive a compensation premium relative to many private sector workers in programs that have been reviewed under the federal government's A-76 program or opened for competition at the state or local government level.[31]

Evidence on the quality of service provided under increased competition is not as complete as the evidence on cost reductions, in part because measuring service quality is inherently more difficult than measuring costs. Available evidence, however, is consistent with the hypothesis that services remain generally satisfactory. Better service is obtained when contract monitoring systems are in place and when contracts adequately specify the tasks and success criteria that will be applied in evaluating quality.

NOTES

1. Wage reductions may stem either from reductions in economic rents or from paying less than competitive wage rates.

2. See, for example, Millward (1982), Frug (1987), AFSCME (1983), and Asher and Popkin (1984).

3. Wage premiums may also be economically efficient if they act as a type of bond that gives employees added incentives to perform assigned functions in settings in which it is difficult to assess performance. See Ippolito (1986) for a discussion. Performance in most positions being considered for increased competition in government commercial services can be monitored and assessed. Hence, the bonding rationale for a wage premium is not generally applicable.

Another explanation for wage premiums is that the employer hires overqualified employees and fails to utilize them fully, but pays the worker as much as he or she could obtain elsewhere. In this scenario, there is no wage premium from the perspective of the individual employee, but there is nonetheless an economic loss to society because the employee is not being utilized in the position is which he or she can make the greatest contribution to production. The hypothesis that government workers are overqualified rather than overpaid may be inconsistent with evidence of low quit rates and large queues of job applicants, such as those observed in the U.S. Postal Service. See Perloff and Wachter (1984), the postal service addendum to chapter 2, and Adie (1977).

4. The effects of excessive prices of goods and services (caused by market power) is the central focus of the antitrust laws enforced by the Federal Trade Commission and the Department of Justice.

Aside from their distortion effects, wage rates either above or below the competitive level are a primarily a matter of income distribution with minimal economic efficiency effects. Higher than competitive wage rates in government represent an income redistribution from taxpayers to government employees rather than a direct real resource loss such as subnormal productivity. Commentators have noted, however, that income redistribution entails real resource loses too, since there are real resource losses associated with raising general revenues. For discussion, see Musgrave and Musgrave (1976, chapter 21), and Seldon (1982).

5. Monopsony in a labor market may occur when there are many sellers (workers) facing a single buyer (employer). Because the monopsonist (employer) realizes that its level of demand for labor substantially affects wage levels, the monopsonist will find it profitable to demand less labor than it would in a competitive market environment. The abnormally low demand of the monopsonist may lead to wages lower than the competitive level. If workers can organize to increase their wages, however, the competitive equilibrium can be restored as wages rise back to the competitive level.

6. An alternative perspective might be that government initially had monopsony power that organized workers have successfully countered. In so doing, organized workers have reestablished the competitive level of wages for government workers and coincidentally improved consumer welfare. Contracting and other forms of increased competition might upset

7. Exploitation of workers may increase short-run productivity at the expense of long-run costs to society. Productivity may be increased in the shortrun by paying such a worker less than a competitive return on his or her investment in expertise and training, since the next best alternative employment may not be related to the accumulated human capital in his or her former job. This is termed a "hold-up." However, in the longrun, workers will be unwilling to undertake this type of investment in specific human capital unless they can be gaurenteed a fair return on their investment. If such guarentees (for example, long-term employment) cannot be made, employers may have to pay a substantial risk premium to attract workers for such jobs. The risk premium will be

necessary to counteract the reputation for exploitation that the employer has acquired.

The potential inefficiencies associated with hold-ups are not limited to job markets. They occur in many long-term relationships between buyers and sellers. For a detailed example and general exposition of the issues, see Gallick (1984).

8. U.S. General Accounting Office (1985a). Increased productivity means providing increased output of services per hour of work. Generally in the A-76 process this means providing the same service with fewer full-time-equivalent (FTE) positions. Increased labor productivity represents a real resource saving because workers no longer required to provide the same service can be transferred to produce valuable services elsewhere in the economy. In contrast, paying lower rates of compensation for the same number of workers is a reduction in transfers from taxpayers to employees. No resources are freed up for use elsewhere in the economy if the workers remain the same except for a reduction in compensation.

9. An annotated listing of selected GAO studies, as well as other studies of the cost effects of privatization on federal, state, and local production costs, are contained in Table 3.2.

10. U.S. General Accounting Office (1981b).

11. GAO attributed this transfer of income from taxpayers to employees to legislation that "cause[s] (5 U.S.C. 5343 (a)) Federal wage rates to exceed local prevailing rates" (U.S. GAO 1981b, p. 6).

If the only reason for cost savings from contracting out under A-76 was that private compensation rates are lower, there should be no cost difference between the initial costs of in-house production and the actual government "bid," which includes efforts to improve efficiency within the context of government production of the service. In fact, there commonly is a substantial difference between the current government costs and the government bid which may reflect reductions in government X-inefficiency and improvements in government organizational structures. See Stolzenberg and Berry (1985) and Musell (1987), for example.

12. Area cleaned per hour was GSA's measure of productivity.

13. The union contract prevented any decrease in the number of private janitors assigned to a building.

14. U.S. General Accounting Office (1981b).

15. If legislated or regulated wage premiums were reduced, the extent of cost savings due to economic rents would be correspondingly reduced. Subsequent cost savings from increased competition would be primarily productivity improvements, i.e., real resource savings.

16. U.S. General Accounting Office (1981d, p. 15).

17. Stolzenberg and Berry (1985).

18. Stolzenberg and Berry (1985, pp. 27-29).

19. Stolzenberg and Berry (1985, pp. 29-30). Both outside costs and in-house costs after reorganization incorporated substantial productivity improvements.

20. Musell (1987, p. 6) and Dudek and Co. (1988, pp. 27-29). Cost minimization (and often equal opportunity guidelines) usually require filling jobs at the lowest grade compatible with satisfactory performance of the job, but some A-76 reviews apparently find that this classification procedure has not been adhered to.

21. DOD's experience suggests that internal efficiency programs divorced from outside competition produce only a quarter to a third of the rate of savings from competitive efficiency reviews (conversations with staff of the Office of Management and Budget charged with reviewing A-76 results, 1987-88).

22. Stevens (1984, pp. 531-34).

23. Characteristics of inherently governmental functions are discussed in chapter 1.

24. Aside from the accountability problem, operation of a central equipment maintenance operation may otherwise be efficient if average costs of equipment maintenance decline as the volume of equipment being maintained increases.

25. For many services, longer shifts reduce the proportion of time spent moving equipment and personnel to the work site or reduce the proportion of time spent on set-up and clean-up even if the total number of hours worked is the same.

26. Stevens (1984, pp. 531-33).

27. See Table 4.1.

28. Stevens (1984, p. 541).

29. The precise calculation in the case of traffic signal maintenance is as follows: The ratio of costs in contract cities relative to costs in in-house cities is 64.1% (column 1). Within the contract cities, the average proportion of costs due to labor is 54% (col. 2). Hence, 34.6 out of 64.1 (64.1 x 0.54) is the cost associated with labor costs, while the remainder, 29.5 (64.1 - 34.6), is due to other types of costs. The compensation rates in the contract cities would be 23.33% higher if they paid at the same rate as in-house cities (column 3). Hence, labor costs would rise to 42.7 (34.6 x 1.2333) if compensation rates were equal in contract and in-house cities and total contract costs would be 72.2% (42.7% + 29.5%) (column 4) of in-house costs. This represents cost savings of 27.8% (100% - 72.2%), after removing the effects of rate of compensation differences (column 5).

30. The 1988 report of the National Commission for Employment Policy (Dudek and Co., 1988) also reviewed evidence on the efficiency and income distribution effects of privatization on many nonpostal services. The commission generally concluded that privatization improves efficiency and also has some income distribution efforts. The magnitude of the income distribution effects, however, are small compared to the concerns expressed by critics of privatization.

31. As noted in Appendix A, although the wage premium itself is a transfer (and therefore its elimination is not directly an efficiency concern), the fact that government-produced services cost more than they would without such transfers may mean that production of these goods is less than it would be otherwise. Less production of these goods will take place unless demand for these services is completely insensitive to price.

5

Conclusions
and Implications

INTRODUCTION

Sole-source, in-house production of government-financed commercial services may entail attenuation of property rights, adoption of unnecessary procedural safeguards, and pursuit of goals unrelated to economic efficiency. All of these conditions may lead to higher costs and a waste of scarce resources. Hence, economists and others have suggested increasing competition as a means of reducing costs. Critics of this proposal argue that the benefits from privatization or other programs to increase competition will produce little in the way of savings because of contractual inadequacies, switching costs, and market failures in procedures used to designate alternative suppliers.[1]

These contending theoretical positions have been tested with clear results. Empirical evidence from numerous studies of costs of production in government-financed commercial services shows there to be substantial cost reductions associated with increased competition over a wide range of activities.

With these empirical estimates of cost savings, total estimated cost savings (both in aggregate and in each level of government and category of spending) from full consideration of increased competition can be produced. This report has gathered estimated rates of cost savings from individual studies and utilized them to produce rough overall estimates of the range of potential cost savings in the United States from increased competition in producing services that the federal government and local and state governments currently produce in-house.

EMPIRICAL ESTIMATES OF COST SAVINGS

The increasing adoption of policies to increase competition in the federal government has made it possible to measure cost savings from these programs. At the federal level, evidence comes predominantly from reviews conducted under the A-76 Circular from the Office of Management and Budget. Both privatization and reorganization of activities reviewed for privatization under the Office of Management and Budget's A-76 procedures consistently have produced savings averaging 30%. If savings at this level were obtained from privatization reviews of the remaining commercial positions in the federal government, the upper bound estimate of annual savings would be approximately $16.6 billion. A low estimate based on earlier studies would be $5.5 billion. An additional $6 to $12 billion in annual savings might be realized by extending increased competition initiatives to the U.S. Postal Service.

At the local and state levels, detailed studies reveal that substantial cost savings are frequently obtained from increased competition in several commercial services. Taking the best available information on cost-savings rates, and applying these rates to in-house production units in state and local governments, results in estimated additional savings of from $14 billion to $55.1 billion annually.

Aggregating the figures from the federal, state, and local government levels, estimated total cost reductions from increasing competition in remaining government-produced commercial services would range from $19.5 billion to $61.7 billion annually, not including the postal service. The present value of such annual total cost savings is $216.7 to $685.6 billion.

The federal and state and local estimates all contain a mixture of efficiency gains and reduced economic rents, in the form of lower rates of compensation. Available evidence indicates that a substantial proportion of total cost savings represent real resource savings. In addition, costs savings that appear to be declines in economic rents may also involve savings in real resources as discussed in chapter 1.[2] There is no evidence that increased competition reduces costs solely by reducing wages. Wide variation occurs from service to service both in the level of budgetary savings and in the proportion of budgetary savings attributable to efficiency gains and reduced economic rents. Using the best available estimates, real resource savings from increased competition could range from 60% to 100% of total cost savings. Assuming the lower figure to be accurate, increased competition would result in real resource savings of between $11.7 billion and $37.2 billion annually. The present value of such a stream of cost savings is $130.0 billion to $413.3 billion.

SUMMARY AND WORLD IMPLICATIONS

A principal characteristic of American economic life is (and has been) pursuit of lower costs and improved quality of goods and services through competition. In the absence of severe market failures, competition provides economically efficient incentives that lead producers to innovate, pay attention to costs and productivity, and charge prices that accurately reflect these costs. Producers that do not provide these benefits to consumers are at a disadvantage compared to those that do and will eventually leave the market.

Over the early 1990s, the practical virtues of markets have been increasingly recognized across the world, but the process of transition from government-operated monopolies to competitive private suppliers is a potentially rocky one.[3] Fortunately, the world is not entirely bereft of experience and data on where to start with increasing competition in government-operated commercial services. Both the United States and other largely market-oriented economies historically have had large portions of their economies subject to government-operation or control. As documented in this study, over the past decade many government-operated commercial services in the United States have moved back into competitive markets of various types. Before the 1970s, most government-financed services were provided by a single in-house agency arguably without effective competition or threat of competition from alternative sources of supply. In many instances, this framework of monopoly in-house production is unlikely to be as efficient as a competitive structure with several potential sources of supply. Fortunately, monopoly in-house production is no longer the only choice available to government decision makers. Recently, more competitive alternatives to in-house government monopolies have been developed and popularized.

The classic economic rationale for government production of a service is that sometimes markets fail to produce enough of a service. Governments have become the producer of last resort for many services that have *appeared* to suffer market failures of some type at some point in history. Governments continue to produce many of these services and have expanded into services where there is little evidence (or even appearance) of market failure.

As economic scholars have investigated the arena of government-produced services more thoroughly, many have become convinced that economic efficiency arguments for government financing of services often do not necessarily justify government production of these services. Admittedly, production of some services is closely tied to issues of government discretion and policymaking and these services likely must be produced within the government and removed from direct competition, other than political competition. For other services, however, the need for production by the government in a monopoly setting seems tenuous, even when a continued need for government intervention is accepted. Further, students of government production have often come to believe that production by monopoly government agencies induces inefficiencies and other forms of higher costs of its own that may be remedied by increased competition. Many of these inefficiencies stem from attenuation of incentives to minimize costs among managers of government agencies.[4] Other inefficiencies may stem from misplaced rules and regulations or extraneous objectives that may disproportionately affect government-produced services.

In the face of evidence that in-house production by government poses efficiency and other cost problems, economists and others have explored alternative competitive production arrangements that might increase incentives to be more cost conscious. There are five prominent forms. The first form is competitive privatization or contracting out. Contracting out involves production by competing private producers of a service that was formerly supplied directly by the government. The second form is intergovernmental competition as described by Tiebot (1956). In this form, competition takes place between governments intent on attracting a larger business tax base, for example. The third form is interagency competition. Here competition is between two or more agencies within the same overall government structure. The Lakewood Plan is a prime example. The fourth form is a mix of private firm and public agency competition in which both types of organizations compete for contracts to provide services to governments. The Phoenix Plan is an example. The fifth form is yardstick competition. Under yardstick competition, private firms compete for the contract to supply one area while government agencies supply other areas. The government agencies receive incentives to meet or beat quality improvements and cost reductions instituted by the private firms.

Each of these forms of governmental competition has theoretical advantages and each has been shown to provide substantial cost savings where it has been implemented. Within the federal government, most of the empirical evidence about the cost savings effects of increased competition comes from studies of defense department operations. A substantial number of services have been converted from in-house production to competitively bid contracts with private suppliers. Other services have been retained in-house, but with substantial savings after internal reorganization. On average, the federal government's competition programs have provided total cost savings averaging 30%.

Outside of the federal government, state and local governments have also been actively involved in utilizing various forms of increased competition to reduce total costs and encourage innovations. Again the evidence indicates substantial potential total cost savings from more widespread adoption of techniques that increase competition. A review of the available studies indicates that total cost savings on state and local services vary considerably from one service to another depending on the characteristics of the service. Services that are easy to define and easy to monitor for quality and price, and that are also widely produced by private firms, make the best candidates for increased competition through outside contracting and other methods. The most substantial total cost savings can be expected from increased competition in such services.   In only a few such services will contracting and monitoring problems be so severe that few total cost saving can be expected. Most commonly, the total cost savings in local and state programs (to increase competition in commercial services currently produced by government) fall in the 20% to 30% range.

What insights from this general summary of U.S. privatization experiences with government-financed services are applicable elsewhere? There is no certain answer, but it is possible to glean some central propositions that are strongly supported by microeconomic theory as well as empirical evidence and that seem likely to be robust over a wide range of institutional settings.

First, there remains a core of services that are inherently governmental and should, therefore, remain the province of government, both with respect to financing and production. Most of these services involve government policymaking, military affairs (but not necessarily military supply), or law enforcement. Even here, competition, between or within government agencies may provide cost savings and quality improvements.

Second, there is a wider circle of services that are at least partially public goods. For these services, government may reasonably continue to arrange financing to help society avoid underproduction. Many of these services, as well as commercial services that the government decides to produce for some other reason, can benefit from competition in their production. The potential benefits include substantially lower production costs, improved quality, and enhanced innovation. The most effective place to start such competition/privatization efforts is services with well-defined and easily measured quality and low minimum efficient scale requirements. In such industries, bids from private entrepreneurial suppliers are more likely to be forthcoming even if there is not a strong tradition of entrepreneurial activity. Further, with such goods and services there is less risk of opportunistic behavior by competing suppliers.

Third, where competition from private parties is less likely to arise (large economies of scale) or is less likely to be appropriate (inherently governmental functions), competition between government units may provide some of the benefits of competition while private enterprise is developing. As private enterprises grow, they can be invited to compete against government agencies for some or all supply opportunities.

Finally, bringing competition to government-financed services through internal reforms is particularly important for society because such services often serve inherently localized markets. As such, it is likely to be more difficult to bring the benefits of competition through other means. For many other goods and services, competition is potentially international or even worldwide in scope. In that case, competitive pricing, quality, and innovation incentives for local suppliers may be introduced into an economy by promoting free trade.[5] There simply is no similar trade alternative for many localized commercial goods and services markets currently supplied by government monopolies.

NOTES

1. Other critics suggest that cost savings will be small because competition between jurisdictions for residents and businesses already creates strong incentives to minimize costs.

2. From an efficiency perspective, it is also important to recognize that transfers (rents) are not costless; they involve real resource losses because raising revenues and making the transfers entail administrative and other costs. Evaluation of administrative costs of taxes and transfers is beyond the scope of this study.

3. See, for example, Humphrey (1990), Koo (1990), Baumol and Lee (1991), Gardelle (1989), Kamm (1991), Auerbach (1991), Mass (1991), and Rudolph (1991).

4. See Thurow (1991) for a vivid description of some of the "cultural" differences between in-house and market production of light bulbs.

5. Baumol and Lee (1991) point out that markets can be quite contestable, even in the face of large absolute economies of scale, if free trade is in effect.

Appendix A

Potential Cost Savings
from Increased Competition

Students of microeconomics have identified two distinct sources of waste that may be attributed to a lack of competition, and that therefore might be expected to arise when production is controlled by a government monopoly. These are (1) allocative inefficiency costs and (2) production inefficiency costs.

Allocative inefficiency occurs when prices are artificially high. As a result, output is lower than the competitive level. Some consumers are no longer willing to purchase the product at the higher price and they consequently are less satisfied than they would have been at the competitive price.[1]

Production inefficiency occurs when more inputs (labor, raw materials, energy, etc.) are used than necessary.[2] Consumers' costs are also raised when so-called "economic rents" are paid to the producers of monopoly services. A rent represents a transfer of income, rather than social waste, but nonetheless reduces consumers' disposable income in favor of the income of the monopolist. Economic rents do cause real waste if real resources are consumed or wasted in the process of collecting taxes to meet the higher costs, if real resources are expended in the course of rent-seeking behavior, or if the higher prices caused by the rent distort the quantity produced.[3]

To explain these different types of costs it is useful to consider the revenue and cost conditions facing a supplier, a government bureau in this case. Figures A.1 and A.2 display demands and costs facing an in-house sole-source monopoly agency. In both figures the demand is that of taxpayers. The supplier is the bureaucracy, and it maximizes rents to those workers lucky enough to retain their jobs when the bureau restricts supply to affect the rent transfers.[4]

In Figure A.1, the demand and marginal revenue curves appear as AP and AM, respectively. Minimum marginal (and average costs) are shown as CO. These are the costs that would prevail under competition. The competitive, socially efficient level of output, DT, is determined by the intersection of the marginal cost and demand curves.

If the bureau or agency acts like a monopolist (restricts supply and increases the price the government has to pay for services), but minimum costs remain the same, the level of output moves from DT to DL. This reduction in output creates a welfare loss because the socially efficient level of output is no longer produced. The allocative efficiency loss is the area of the triangle IKO in Figure A.1. This area represents the loss of value to consumers from the reduction in output.

Figure A.1
Allocative Inefficiency and Rents Due to Monopoly

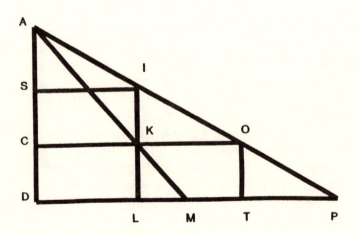

In Figure A.1, increased consumer costs due to monopoly power of the bureau are represented by CKIS. If prices are increased exclusively by paying higher prices for the same raw materials, management, or labor, the area CKIS represents a transfer from consumers to producers (i.e., an economic rent), rather than a social loss, because it does not disturb production decisions in other sectors of the economy. Nothing is wasted or used that would not otherwise be used in producing output DL.

Increased competition would prevent the bureau from exercising market power and would therefore eliminate both the rent and the misallocation of resources. The attenuated property rights hypothesis is consistent with the conditions depicted in Figure A.1, but it is also consistent with the subsequent figure.

Figure A.2 repeats all basic elements in Figure A.1 but adds the possibility that lack of competition will permit greater than necessary use of resources. Figure A.2 could be interpreted as the effect of a bureau that works to increase the number of employees (or works to retain employees in the face of efficiency-enhancing technical change or lower demand). Underutilization of labor of this type represents a real resource loss.[5] This can be represented by a shift in the average (and marginal) cost curve from CO to BN. If this occurs, the "competitive" output (with increased costs) will be reduced to DW. The area BCVN represents increased use of resources, such as more equipment or more hours of labor to accomplish a given task. All of BCVN is social loss. Resources are being consumed that could otherwise produced other services that would satisfy consumers. The allocative inefficiency loss in Figure A.2 is NVO. And BCVN can be used to present the effects of X-inefficiency, additional goals, and excessive rules. All three cost increases result in high per unit utilization of real resources. Given constant demand, this waste of resources also causes an allocative efficiency loss. Increased competition in the context of Figure A.2 would force the agency to reduce its costs or be displaced by a supplier with lower costs (less waste of resources).

A combination of monopoly power and inefficient production costs is also possible and this combines the effect in Figures A.1 and A.2.

Figure A.2
Resource Waste from Excessive Costs

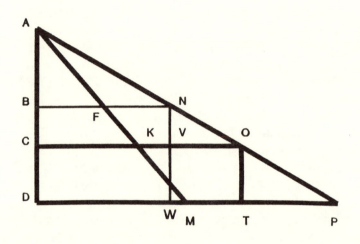

NOTES

1. Allocative inefficiency also occurs when prices are below the competitive level. In this case, too much of the low-priced good is produced and not enough of other goods.

2. If production inefficiency results in higher prices, it will also cause allocative inefficiency.

3. Distortion of this type will accompany economic rents unless demand is completely inelastic.

4. This is a seniority model in which the workers with job security determine the bureau's level of output exclusively for their own benefit and at the expense of workers with little job security who will be fired as the bureau reduces output to increase benefits for the remaining workers.

5. This discussion assumes that each hour of labor contains a potential level of effort that may or may not be utilized. However, if it is not utilized, it cannot be somehow retrieved later. Hence, an hour of employment that does not utilize all of a worker's available effort represents a loss to society because the same worker in another employment context would provide his or her full effort.

Appendix B

Turf Maintenance Services: An Example of the Stevens (1984) Study Methodology

INTRODUCTION

This condensed excerpt indicates the kind of detailed examination of technologies and conditions that characterizes the Stevens (1984) study.[1] Its attention to detail and direct measurement of inputs, community characteristics, and service quality sets it apart from many other studies that have had to rely on secondary information sources and indirect observations. The considerable weight placed on the results of the Stevens (1984) study in this and other reviews of empirical cost savings studies stems from these major advantages. The regression results from the Stevens (1984) study are used in the summary of cost savings statistics in this study because the regression technique does the best job of taking into account and controlling for all of the relevant cost factors.

DISCUSSION OF SERVICE

Turf maintenance is generally considered to be part of parks and public grounds maintenance. It can be defined as the maintenance of grassy areas in parks, along median strips and other grounds abutting public roadways, and surrounding public buildings.

Mowing is the major task associated with turf maintenance. It takes place with varying frequency and with varying sized crew and equipment. Depending on the season and the need, crews will also then engage in weeding, edging clipping, fertilizing, seeding, and spraying.

Level of service is related to the frequency of mowing as well as to the type of turf being maintained and its intensity of use. [G]olf courses and other types of special lawns will require more frequent mowing than parklands being kept in a wild state.   It should be noted that too frequent mowing may not necessarily be coincident with a high level of service. In overcutting the grass, one may hamper its ability to retain moisture. The rate of growth of the grass species will also dictate frequency of mowing. Other factors or conditions [that] affect service delivery are annual rainfall and the ease to which the terrain lends itself to maintenance. For example, hilly turf areas are more difficult to mow than flat turf areas.

Scale of operations can be defined as number of acres maintained or mowed by the service provider. One would expect that the larger the areas to be mowed and maintained, the more likely would be the use of large mowing machines and other mechanized equipment. In addition, one would expect that the greater the number of areas to be maintained, the higher the cost of delivering the service.

DEFINITIONS AND MEASUREMENT

The underlying purpose of this analysis is to determine whether organizational arrangement (municipal or contract) has a significant impact on cost, maintaining equal quality and providing identical levels of service. In order to perform this analysis, two different analytical approaches are taken. The first approach is a matched pair analysis.

The second analytical technique, multiple regression, examines the impact of organizational arrangement on cost of service delivery. Initially all factors outside the managers' or cities' control, as well as service level, will be held constant. As a second level of analysis, management factors will be examined. Of particular interest is the interaction of management factors and organizational arrangement, should organizational arrangement prove to be significantly related to service cost. The remainder of this section discusses the specific variables which are used in the analysis. The variables are summarized in Table B.1[2]

Cost

Cost is computed as the sum of direct and indirect costs attributed to turf management. For a municipally serviced city, cost is defined as the sum of direct salaries attributed to turf management, fringe benefits associated with these salaries, other than personnel operating expenses (which include office expenses, insurance expenses, and utilities), and capital equipment expenditures. Capital equipment expenditures include maintenance labor and parts as well as depreciation.

In turf management, equipment was depreciated over five years on a straight line basis, with the exception of tractors, which were depreciated over seven years. In addition, overhead, defined as a portion of general government functions such as personnel, budget, and finance, was allocated to the service. In the contract cities, costs consisted of payments to the contractor and all associated municipal contract monitoring costs. Direct salary, fringe benefit, equipment as well as general governmental expenditures (overhead) associated with the contract were included.

For purposes of the study, general government overhead was computed by two methods, each having its pros and cons. By the first method, the ratio of direct municipal salaries (attributable to turf management) to total direct municipal salaries was obtained. This percentage was applied against total salaries and other than personnel expenses for general government agencies such as planning, budget, and personnel. By the second method, the ratio of total costs for the service (exclusive of overhead) to the total city expense budget was obtained. This percentage was then applied to personnel and nonpersonnel expenditures of "general" government agencies.

The first method works best when the amount of time spent by an overhead agency on a particular service can be defended as being closely related to the number of workers delivering the direct service.

Table B.1
**Summary of Measures Used for Cost, Scale of Operation,
Level/Condition of Service, Quality, Technology,
Managament, Efficiency, and Demographics**

Factor	Measures	Variable
Cost	1. Total cost of turf maintenance (calculating overhead based on municipal salaries) 2. Total cost of turn maintenance (calculating overhead based on total expenditure on service)("G&A" method) * Figure does not include cost of water	T1 T2
Scale of Opera- tion	1. Number of turn areas maintained 2. Annual acres mowed 3. Total number of parks 4. Annual frequency of different activities performed (weeding, aerating, fertilizing, watering, seeding) by service provider	S1 S2 S3 L2
Level/ Con- dition of Service	1. Intensity of use factor 2. Frequency of mowing (annual) 3. Annual rainfall (inches) 4. Percentage of terrain which presents no problems 5. Percentage of terrain which presents diffi- culties 6. Total ballfields, special lawns and play- grounds	C1 C2 C3 C4 C5 C6
Quality	1. Average quality rating 2. Percentage of areas receiving other than "Excellent" rating	Q1 Q2

Table B.1 (continued)

Factor	Measures	Variable
Man-age-ment	1. Average age of crewpersons 2. Average tenure of crewpersons 3. Average crew size 4. Absenteeism (included sick days, vacation days and holidays) 5. Are workers unionized? 6. Are supervisors responsible for crews working in more than one location? 7. Do periodic staff meetings take place? 8. Can supervisors hire workers? 9. Can supervisors fire workers? 10. Are written reprimands given to denote unsatisfactory work? 11. Aver monthly wage of direct labor.	M4 M6 M3 M7 M8 M2 M9 M11 M12 M13 Wage
Tech-nology	1. Number of lawnmowers per crewperson	M14
Effi-ciency	1. Cost per acre mowed (overhead based on municipal salaries) 2. Cost per acre mower (overhead based on total expenditures on service) 3. Cost per acre maintained (overhead based on municipal salaries) 4. Cost per acre maintained (overhead based on total expenditures on service) 5. Full-time equivalent hours per acre mowed.	CPAM1 CPAM2 TOT-AC1 TOT-AC2 FT-EPAM
Demo-graph-ics	1. Population 2. Median household income	POP MED

The second "G & A method" works best in those situations in which an overhead agency's involvement is related to total expenditures rather than to the amount and salary level of employees.

Scale of Operation

Scale of operations is defined as the total number of acres of turf maintained by the service provider.[3] Another scale variable will be aggregate annual frequency at which an array of turf management functions (e.g., seeding, edge clipping, etc.) is conducted.

Quality of Service

Service quality, for the purposes of this study, was determined by observer ratings of turf on a number of different variables. In each city, the three largest parks were selected. Up to ten observation areas were randomly selected in each park. In some cases, parks were too small to obtain ten observation areas; thus, fewer than ten observation areas were obtained. Each observation area comprised a turf-covered section of approximately 100 by 100 feet. Turf was rated for quality of edging, grass height, grass color, extent of weeds and extent of uniform cover. Ratings were scaled 1 to 4 where 1 = excellent and 4 = poor. Table B.2 lists the codes and definitions of the turf quality ratings.[4] From these quality ratings several variables were obtained. These included an overall quality average (QI) derived from averaging ratings over each dimension for each of the thirty observation areas. The other quality variable (Q2) was derived from the number of areas receiving an other than excellent rating (or "1") on any of the five dimensions. In addition, averages of quality ratings on each separate dimension were computed.

Table B.2
Explanation of Ratings and Codes

Ratings for Edging Work

1 = Excellent: Grass cut smoothly at sidewalk's edge, distinct straight line.
2 = Good: Grass beginning to grow into edged areas, although it has not grown more than 1/2"
3 = Fair: Grass has grown 1" into edged area
4 = Poor: Grass has grown more than 1" into edged area

Ratings for Grass Color

1 = Medium Green
2 = Light Green
3 = Yellow Green
4 = Brown

Ratings for Grass Height

1 = .5" - 1.5"
2 = 1.5" - 2.5"
3 = 2.5" - 4"
4 = 4" - 6"

Ratings for Weeds

1 = Excellent: No weeds found in observation area
2 = Good: Weeds found in 10% or less of observation area
3 = Fair: Weeds found in 10% to one-third of observation area
4 = Poor: Weeds found in more than one-third of observation area

Ratings for % of Grass Cover

1 = 100% to 75%
2 = 75% to 50%
3 = 50% to 25%
4 = 25% to 0%

Technology and Managerial Factors

There are various factors directly related to management that may affect the cost or performance of personnel. These include: degree of supervision, wage rates, degree of unionization, type of supervision, age and tenure of workers, absenteeism, and size of crew. More specifically, under type of supervision, variables include: whether or not supervisors are responsible for crews working in more than one location, whether or not periodic staff meetings take place, whether or not supervisors can hire or fire workers, and whether or not written reprimands are given to laborers to denote unsatisfactory work. Managerial factors can have a mixed impact on cost.

Technology of turf maintenance is related to the number of automated pieces of equipment used by a crew. In most cases, the more automated equipment that is used, the higher the productivity of workers.

Efficiency Measures

Two basic performance measures will be included. These are (1) the cost per acre of turf mowed and (2) full-time equivalent employees per acre of turf mowed. Initially, the output measure to be used was acres of turf maintained. It was found that this output measure caused problems since it did not take into account any consideration of the frequency of the activity. In contrast, acres of turf mowed consists of acres mowed multiplied by the frequency of mowing. This measure gives a more accurate indication of the amount of work being done. Cost per acre mowed is a self-evident variable. Full-time equivalent employees per acre mowed may be an indicator of productivity. Too many employees working per acre would result in high cost despite low levels of output. On the other hand, a municipality that uses few employees per mowed acre may show high efficiency.

REGRESSION ANALYSIS

General Results

It is quite possible that scale, level, and organizational arrangement have a joint effect on costs. An analysis of these joint effects can be best examined through a multivariate statistical technique. Using multiple regression, an equation is calculated which predicts the total cost of turf maintenance as a function of scale, level of service, and organizational arrangement. The basic format of the equation to be estimated makes the assumption that [the] scale, level, and conditions of service are beyond the control of management as a result of political, topographical, or other reasons. Furthermore, organizational arrangement embodies those factors (such as crew size, use of equipment, vacation policies, supervisory policies) that are within management's control. If it is found that organizational arrangement significantly affects costs (controlling for scale, level and condition of service), then further analysis can be performed to determine which management and technology factors are contributing to the difference in cost found between municipal and contract systems.

Table B.3 presents the results of the regression analysis. The total cost of turf maintenance is the dependent variable. Total costs are calculated using overhead method two.[5]

Total cost was regressed against measures of scale (number of acres maintained, number of acres mowed per year, number of parks, number of different activities performed), level of service (frequency of mowing on an annual basis, city conditions (percent of the terrain having no problems), and a dummy variable (0 = contract, 1 = municipal) for organizational arrangement. The preferred equation reported as equation #1 includes as independent variables, total acres mowed per year, total number of different activities performed by the service provider, percent of area with no problems, and organizational arrangement.[6]

Equation #2 in Table B.3 adds a variable representing the quality of turf maintenance to the basic cost equation. Quality is included as the average overall quality rating.

Table B.3
Regression Results (Dependent Variable = Total Costs of Turf Maintenance Services)

Independent Variable (Mean)	Equation #1 without Quality Coefficient (t-statistic)	Equation #2 with Quality Coefficient (t-statistic)
Constant	3.03	3.36
Organizational Arrangement 1 = Municipal; 0 = Contract	.33 (2.06)B	.34 (2.09)B
Acres mowed per year (LNS2) (7.0798)	.89 (8.41)A	.89 (8.12)A
Number of different activities performed by service provider (LNS2) (7.0798)	.39 (2.71)A	.37 (2.40)A
% of terrain with no problems (LNC4) (2.092)	-.12 (2.97)A	-.12 (2.74)A
Quality Rating (LNQ1) (.5116)		-.21 (.56)
R^2 F(k-1,n-k) Standard error Number of observations	.83 4,15 = 24.23A .35 20	.82 5,14 = 18.68B .35 20

NOTE: A = Significant at the 95% confidence level.
B = Significant at the 90% confidence level.

Table B.4
Regression Results Including Management Factors
(Logarithmic Form)

Independent Variable (Mean)	Equation Coefficient (t-statistic)
Constant	2.11
Organizational Arrangement 1 = Municipal; 0 = Contract	.52 (1.94)B
Acres mowed per year (LNS2) (7.7089)	.84 (9.26)A
Different activities performed per year (LNC2) (5.5940)	.71 (4.77)A
Average overall quality (LNQ1) (.5116)	-.36 (1.18)
Terrain with no problems (LNCH) (2.0912)	-.21 (5.15)A
Are workers unionized (LNMS) 1 = yes; 0 = no	1.17 (3.24)A
Are supervisors responsible for crews at different locations (LNM2) 1 = yes; 0 = no	-.92 (2.92)A
Can supervisor fire workers (LNM9) 1 = yes; 0 = no	.74 (2.36)A
Do periodic staff meetings take place (LNM11) 1 = yes; 0 = no	.46 (1.78)
R^2 F(k-1,n-k) Standard error Number of observations	.90 9,10 = 20.11A .26 20

NOTE: A = Significant at the 95% confidence level.
B = Significant at the 90% confidence level.

On average, holding constant number of acres mowed per year, different types of activities performed, percentage of terrain with no problems, organizational arrangement, and quality of service, municipal delivery of turf maintenance services is 40% more costly than contract delivery.

Regression Analysis - Management and Technology Factors

In order to determine which relevant management and technology factors might also be affecting costs, several stepwise regressions were calculated.[7] Table B.4 shows the results of adding management factors stepwise to the cost equation. Unionization and the extent to which supervisors are responsible for crews working in different locations have the most significant impact on costs. Unionization is associated with higher costs. With the addition of the unionization variable to the cost equation, organizational arrangement ceases to have a significant impact on costs. Next in significance as a management variable is whether supervisors are responsible for crews in different locations. Examination of the t-tests and the regression results points to a central finding: in turf maintenance activities, municipalities tend to have a more structured work environment than do contractors.

The strong linkage between organizational arrangement and management factors is underscored by another regression analysis in which organizational arrangement was regressed against management and condition factors in a stepwise fashion. One variable, the absentee rate, was associated with 77% of the variation between municipal and contract. With four variables, absentee rate, percentage of terrain with no problems, supervisory ability to hire workers, and vacation days per worker one can predict organizational arrangement with a high degree of accuracy ($R = .93$). This regression has implications for the conduct of municipal managers. If municipalities can reduce absenteeism, restructure their vacation packages, and allow more flexibility in personnel practices, permitting supervisors more direct control, they can lower their costs without affecting the level and quality of services delivered.

NOTES

1. This appendix is excerpted from B. Stevens, *Delivering Municipal Services Efficiently: A Comparison of Municipal and Private Service Delivery* (Washington, D.C.: U.S. Department of Housing and Urban Development, 1984), 370-408.

2. Not all of these variables can be utilized in the main regressions because of the limitations of the sample size. When the number of explanatory variables had to be reduced for this reason, the technique used was to select from each category of explanatory variables, the one with the most explanatory power. This selection was done by stepwise regressions.

Ideally, the variable selected in this fashion will covary with the other variables in the category so that it effectively "represents" the whole category in the regression.

Ideally, intensity of use covaries with "percentage of terrain which presents no problems." In this instance, it does not seem unreasonable to posit that difficult terrain gets less use.

Using a principal components approach would have been an alternative method in the circumstances.

Both of these procedures, however, result in specification error and resulting unknown bias in the coefficients.

3. Acres of turf mowed was also used because the acres maintained variable did not account for differences in the number of times mowing occurred. Cost variables were also put on a cost per acre mowed basis for the same reason.

4. These quality ratings were obtained from field observations of grass height taken on randomly selected parcels of park land in each jurisdiction. They are not based on mower heights or other input measures.

It is possible that maintenance practices of previous providers could bias the quality measure. There is no indication that the sample cities had recently converted from municipal agency to contract form of production or the reverse, so this effect, if any, should not be substantial.

5. Both a linear and logarithmic version of the equation were tested.

6. The variable, percentage of terrain with no problems, was selected from among three other condition variables including annual rainfall, intensity of use of parks, and total number of different types of parks. When included in a step-wise regression with total cost as the dependent variable, the above variable consistently appeared as most significant.

7. In stepwise regression, a list of possible independent variables is specified. These variables are added to the estimating equation, one by one, according to the amount of variance in the dependent variable explained. Thus the first variable to be added to the estimating equation

is the variable that has the greatest correlation with the dependent variable.

Appendix C

Main Quality of Service Findings and Reasons for Observed Cost Differences in the Stevens (1984) Study

---

Service Name, Quality Measures, and Reasons for Cost Differences

---

Janitorial Services

*   There is virtually no difference in the quality. On a scale of 1 = cleanest to 3 = dirtiest, contractors rated an average of 1.65 while municipal agencies rated an average 1.66.

*   Contractors, as compared to municipal agencies, tend (1) to pay lower wages and fringes, (2) to use part-time workers, (3) to schedule cleaning during nonbusiness hours, (4) to employ more equipment, and (5) to achieve a lower absentee rate. The factors most closely associated with low cleaning costs are wage rates and cleaning schedules.

Refuse Collection

*   Quality of refuse collection service varied from 11.05 (best) to 92.7 (worst), with an average value of 34.3 for the municipal cities and 38.2 for the contract cities. Thus, the average quality is almost identical.

Service Name, Quality Measures, and Reasons for Cost Differences

Refuse Collection (continued)

*   In comparison to municipal agencies, contractors are able to achieve lower absentee rates (7.9% versus 13.4%) and vehicle downtime ratios (6.2% of the contractor versus 16.2% of municipal vehicles are in the garage for repair, on average, at any time); contractors are more likely to operate fleets with a single brand of equipment (more efficient parts and repair); and contractor workers are more likely to make two loads per truck shift than are municipal workers.

Payroll Processing

*   There is no difference in the quality of payroll services between contract and in-house cities.

*   Cities with the lowest costs of payroll preparation tend (1) to achieve lower absenteeism; (2) to have a younger workforce; (3) not to reward workers with bonuses for suggestions;[1] (4) to have the contractor sign the check if the service is contracted out; (5) not to have the data processing division in the same department as payroll; (6) to pay a smaller percentage of all municipal workers on an hourly as compared to salaried basis; (7) to have lower error rates in paychecks; and (8) to have slightly less speedy payroll preparation. Contract payroll operations were neither more nor less likely to have these characteristics than in-house payroll operations.

Traffic Signal Maintenance

*   Municipal cities get to repairs faster (37 versus 43 minutes), but take longer to make the repair (77 versus 37 minutes) than contract cities. The net result is that there is no significant difference.

*   The reasons that municipal cities have higher costs include:
        1. Municipal cities take longer to complete repairs. (They have no backup crews and, if unable to complete a repair due to lack of parts or equipment, they must go and get it and return to complete the repair).

Service Name, Quality Measures, and Reasons for Cost Differences

---

Traffic Signal Maintenance (continued)

2. Municipal cities spend more time in a response mode rather than in a preventive one. Municipal cities allocate less time to preventive maintenance and perform significantly fewer preventive maintenance checks or activities.

3. Municipal systems have fewer solid state signals, are less likely to be controlled by computers, are older, and are repaired less often by crews specially designed vehicles. Municipal systems have older and generally less sophisticated systems and therefore repairs are more serious and take longer to make.

4. Municipal systems have less productive workers. Each contractor repairman maintains 70 intersections compared to 43 intersections per municipal repairman.

Asphalt Overlay

*   There is no significant difference in the quality of service provided by contractors and that provided by municipal agencies. Using a rating system modified after one developed by the Asphalt Institute, asphalt overlays put down by contractors had an average rating of 97.2 (out of a perfect score of 100), whereas those put down by municipal agencies had an average rating of 94.9.

*   Most of the differences appear to be explained by five factors (1) higher productivity - contractor crews put down more tons of asphalt per man-day; (2) technology - contractors use pavers with larger paving widths and heavier rollers; (3) management - contractors assign larger crews to an overlay project than do municipal agencies; (4) supervision of workers - contractor foremen are more likely to remain on-site directing operations continuously and are also more likely to have the authority to fire workers; and (5) responsibility for equipment maintenance - contractors are more likely to be responsible for equipment maintenance. Contractor crewmen are also paid significantly more than comparable municipal employees.

Service Name, Quality Measures, and Reasons for Cost Differences

---

Turf Maintenance

*   The quality of turf maintenance services was about 7% higher in the contract cities compared with the municipal cities according to an average quality of service rating. This difference, however, was not statistically significant.

*   The major factor explaining this cost difference is worker remuneration. Municipal workers receive salaries and fringe benefits averaging $20,866, whereas the contractors' workers received $13,686.

A major component of the difference is fringe benefits - municipal agencies pay over 40% and contractors pay just under 20% of salaries as fringe benefits.

The higher cost of turf maintenance services in the ten municipal cities compared with the ten contract cities also may be explained, in part, by the following managerial factors: (1) absenteeism rates - the municipal turf maintenance workers show much higher absentee rates (which includes vacation time) than contract workers; (2) tenure and unionization - municipal workers are significantly more likely than contract workers to be older, employed for a longer period of time, and members of unions; (3) supervision of laborers - contractors have greater flexibility than municipalities in supervision practices such as hiring and firing workers.

Street Tree Maintenance

*   The quality of street tree maintenance services in the contract and municipal cities is virtually identical. The average quality of service rating (reflecting tree safety, quality of pruning cuts, and general health of street trees as determined by a professional arborist), using a four point rating scale (1 = excellent and 4 = poor) was 1.94 in the municipal cities and 2.02 in the contract cities. This difference was not statistically significant.

*   A number of management factors appear to explain the difference in the cost of contract and municipal street tree services. They include:
(1) personnel costs - the mean salary and fringe benefit rates of contract laborers are somewhat lower than equivalent municipal workers;

Service Name, Quality Measures, and Reasons for Cost Differences

---

Street Tree Maintenance (continued)

(2) absentee rates - the municipal street tree maintenance workers are absent more often than contract laborers (vacation absences are included in this calculation);
(3) tenure and unionization - the municipal street tree maintenance workers are significantly older and show higher lengths of employment and percentages of union membership than contract workers;
(4) supervision - municipal workers have significantly more levels of supervisors between themselves and top management personnel and contract supervisors have more flexibility than municipal supervisors in regard to hiring and firing laborers; and
(5) equipment maintenance - contractors are significantly more likely than municipal street tree maintenance departments to be responsible for equipment maintenance.

NOTE

1. Bonuses for suggestions are usually associated with lower costs. It may be that payroll processing is so routinized that suggestions for additional improvements do not produce sufficient savings to offset the cost of the awards.

Appendix D

Additional Insights from a More Recent Study of Florida Local Government

One replication of the International City Management Association (ICMA) survey has been conducted in conjunction with a 1987 study of privatization in Florida.[1] Comparing the ICMA's 1982 responses from Florida with later responses from Florida, the authors found similar levels of privatization, although they concluded that privatization had increased in Florida over the period between studies. The average number of privatized services increasing from 10.1 to 12.8 out of 57 service categories studied.[2]

Aside from confirming the general levels of privatization and other forms of competition adopted by local governments, the Florida survey also provides some evidence about the relationship between types of services and changes in privatization rates. The overall upward trend in privatization of local government services found in Florida subsumes quite different trends in privatization in different categories of government services. Strong increases appear in the public works, transportation, and general government support categories. These are service categories with fairly well defined output measures and stable technologies. In the ICMA's terminology, these categories are composed primarily of "hard services" or tangible services where contracts specifying specific outputs are fairly easy to draw up and are common in the private sector.[3] In terms of the discussion of vertical integration in chapter 1, these are services categories in which markets, rather than in-house production, often work best. To the extent that other services can be structured to include well-defined outputs that are commonly produced by private firms, other services may also make good candidates for contracting and the ICMA's listing is too restrictive. Similarly, characteristics of some communities or the organization of government in these communities may make additional categories of services promising areas for increased competition through contracting.

In less well-defined and measured service categories, the pattern over time in rates of privatization in Florida appears to be different. In the "public safety" category, for example, privatization levels were stagnant. Levels of privatization for "soft" service categories such as "health and human services" declined. Within service categories such as "parks and recreation," differences in trends are observable. Although privatization in the "parks and recreation" area as a whole declined, the "routine maintenance services" within the category showed increasing privatization. These findings highlight the fact that the overall budget categories from the census combine services and that potential savings rates in different services within a service category may not be identical to the average savings rate for the category.

The strong trend toward increased privatization of government services and the difference in patterns between "hard" and "soft" spending categories suggests that local governments in Florida perceive there to be advantages in adopting privatization where services are well defined and easy to measure. The fact that this trend has developed and accelerated in an era of increased budget stringency is consistent with that hypothesis that selective privatization provides cost savings. These savings are likely to available in most communities in "hard" services categories, although many communities may obtain savings in other types of services as well.

NOTES

1. Clarkson and Fixler (1987). Their survey was conducted in 1986. Although Hinds (1991) relies on a much smaller survey sample, the study concludes that privatization trends have continued unabated. Also see Carlson (1991).

2. Clarkson and Fixler (1987, p. 169). Florida's rate of privatization was slightly lower than the national average in the 1982 ICMA study (18.6% versus 19.5%). If the relative relationship between privatization in Florida and the United States held constant over the period, the national figure for 1986 would be 13.4 of 57 services, or 23.5%.

Substantial growth in privatization also was found in comparing a 1973 survey with the 1982 survey. Increases ranged from 43% for refuse collection to 3,644% for data processing. See Fixler and Poole (1987, pp. 164-178).

3. The ICMA gives the following as examples of hard services: solid waste collection, solid waste disposal, street repair, road striping, street cleaning, snow removal, parking lot operation, vehicle towing and storage, parks maintenance tree trimming, animal control, payroll, tax billing, tax assessing, sludge disposal, street light maintenance, utility meter reading, and utility billing. Examples of "soft" services include: crime prevention/ patrol, fire prevention, emergency preparedness, civil defense, recreational services, child welfare programs, elderly programs, alcohol and substance abuse programs, public health programs, mental health facilities, legal services, personnel services, labor relations, and public relations.

Appendix E

Census, ICMA,
and Research Categories

INTRODUCTION

The goal of this appendix is to describe the trail of decisions associated with the cost-savings estimates for each expenditure category from the census of governments.

As described in the text, the process of producing the cost-savings estimates requires integrating several data sources. Census materials provide total expenditures for clusters of services. The International City Managment Association survey in Valente and Manchester (1984) indicates how extensively traditional in-house monopoly production is still utilized in individual services. These individual service results are aggregated to correspond to the census categories. The ICMA results (aggregated to the census categories) are used to estimate the proportion of the census total expenditures that are produced in-house for each individual service category in the census. Research results from various studies provide the estimated potential rates of cost savings expected to be realized from introducing more competition in supplying services that are currently provided on a monopolized in-house basis. These savings rates are multiplied by the estimates of in-house expenditures to produce the overall savings estimates.

Different data sets use different definitions of individual services or include (or exclude) different services that are components of the census categories. Data sets also frequently aggregate services in different ways. Therefore, integration of data sets necessarily involves imperfect matches between categories. Five elements in this matching process are discussed below.

RELIANCE ON DESCRIPTIVE TITLES OF SERVICES

In the case of the ICMA survey results and some of the cost-savings estimates, no specific definitions of services are available. However, these sources do provide information on many apparently narrow government services categories, which appear by their titles to be components of the broader census categories.

A RANGE OF ESTIMATES USED

The two cost-savings estimates, "base" and "high," were determined as follows: The "base" estimate represents a cautious, but not unduly pessimistic, estimate of potential cost-savings rates. It is derived from individual cost savings studies listed in Table 3.2. It includes the lowest cost estimate among the studies pertaining to the category, unless a cost-savings estimate from Stevens (1984) is available for use. Using the lowest estimate in all cases would be unduly pessimistic where there is a highly detailed study (that controls for quality and other factors) to provide a more reliable estimate, in particular, the study by Stevens (1984). The "high" estimate represents an optimistic, but still realistic, estimate of potential cost savings. The "high" estimated cost-savings rate for a service category consists of the upper bound estimate from the Clarkson and Fixler (1987) literature review, unless one of the individual studies in Table 3.2 provides a higher cost-savings estimate. Whenever the Clarkson and Fixler (1987) cost-savings estimates are used and several services covered by Clarkson and Fixler are components of the more broadly defined census expenditure category, the average savings rate for the services from Clarkson and Fixler is used for the "high" estimate.

Table E.1
Concordance of Research Categories

Census Expenditure Category, Census Definition, ICMA Category or
Categories, Research Categories, and Discussion of the
Correspondence Among Categories from Different Sources

AIRPORTS:

Census Definition: Construction, maintenance, operation, and
support of airport facilities.

ICMA category: Operation of Airports.

Research category (base): Airports. See Table 3.2, service category
2.

Research category (high): Airport Management and Control Tower
Maintenance (40%). See Clarkson and Fixler (1987, Table IV-1, pp. 172-
75).

Correspondence: The match of categories appears to be good
except that airport capital outlays are included only in the census data.
Current operations account for 47% of total expenditures in the census
category.[1]   Evidence about the effects of increased competition on
construction costs (see housing) suggests that cost savings could be
expected from the capital outlay portion of airport expenditures. However,
to be conservative, cost-savings estimates are based solely on the
operating cost portion of airport expenditures reported in the census.

Census Expenditure Category, Census Definition, ICMA Category or
Categories, Research Categories, and Discussion of the
Correspondence Among Categories from Different Sources

FINANCIAL ADMINISTRATION:

Census Definition: Officials and agencies concerned with tax
assessment and collection, accounting, auditing, budgeting, purchasing,
custody of funds, and other central finance activities.

ICMA categories: Payroll, Tax Bill Processing, Tax Assessing, and
Delinquent Tax Collection.

Research category (base): Assessment, Property Tax, Payroll and
Data Processing. See Table 3.2, service categories 4 and 28.

Research category (high): Payroll (36%), Tax Bill Processing (36%),
Assessment (36%), Delinquent Tax Collection (30%). See Clarkson and
Fixler (1987, Table IV-1, pp. 172-75.[2]

Correspondence: The match among the census and ICMA categories
appears to be good. The base research category, however, is not as
inclusive as the other data sources.

The zero cost-savings estimates from the payroll research category
are used for the base savings estimates, even though cost savings greater
than zero were found for the "assessment" research category. Hence, the
base cost-savings calculations are likely to be a conservative estimate of
the cost-savings rate for the census cluster of services. The high cost-
savings rate estimate is the mean of the rates for the four separate
services covered by Clarkson and Fixler (1987).

Current expenditures constitute more than 95% of total expenditures.
Evidence about the effects of increased competition on construction costs
(see housing) suggests that cost savings could be expected from the
capital outlay portion of airport expenditures.   However, to be
conservative, cost-savings estimates are based solely on the operating
cost portion of expenditures reported in the census.

Census Expenditure Category, Census Definition, ICMA Category or Categories, Research Categories, and Discussion of the Correspondence Among Categories from Different Sources

FIRE PROTECTION:

Census Definition: Fire fighting organization and auxiliary service, fire inspection and investigation; support of volunteer fire forces; and other fire prevention activities. Includes cost of fire fighting facilities, such as fire hydrants and water, furnished by other agencies of the government.

ICMA category: Fire Prevention and Suppression.

Research category (base): Fire Protection. See Table 3.2, service category 11.

Research category (high): Fire Protection. See Kristensen (1983) and Hilke (1986) in Table 3.2, service category 11.

Correspondence: The match of categories appears to be good.
Operating expenditures account for 93% of total costs. However, since the research categories include consideration of capital inputs, the cost-savings estimates are based on total expenditures.

Census Expenditure Category, Census Definition, ICMA Category or Categories, Research Categories, and Discussion of the Correspondence Among Categories from Different Sources

GENERAL MAINTENANCE OF PUBLIC BUILDINGS:

Census Definition: Provision and maintenance of public buildings not allocated to particular functions.

ICMA categories: Buildings and Grounds Maintenance, Building Security.

Research category (base): Cleaning Services, Security Services. See Table 3.2, service categories 7 and 37.

Research category (high): Cleaning Services and Building and Ground Maintenance (42%), Building Security (59%). See Clarkson and Fixler (1987, Table IV-1, pp. 172-175.

Correspondence: The match appears to be good.

The Stevens (1984) estimate of the base cost-savings rate is used for the whole category even though the reported cost-savings rate for security services is higher. Hence the base cost-savings calculation is a conservative estimate of potential cost savings.

Current operations account for 61% of total expenditures. Evidence about the effects of increased competition on construction costs (see housing) suggests that cost savings could be expected from the capital outlay portion of airport expenditures. However, to be conservative, cost-savings estimates are based solely on the operating cost portion of the census category total.

Census Expenditure Category, Census Definition, ICMA Category or Categories, Research Categories, and Discussion of the Correspondence Among Categories from Different Sources

HEALTH SERVICES:

Census Definition: Out-patient health services, other than hospital care, including: public health administration; research and education; categorical health programs; treatment and immunization clinics; nursing environmental health activities such an air and water pollution control; ambulance service if provided separately from fire protection services; and other general public health activities such as mosquito abatement.[3] Also includes financing, construction, and operations of nursing homes. School health services provided by health agencies (rather than school agencies) are included here.

ICMA category: Public Health Programs.

Research categories (base): Health Services, Nursing Homes. See Table 3.2, service categories 13 and 25.

Research category (high): Public Health Program Management (40%), Drug and Alcohol Treatment Programs (40%), Operation and Management of Mental Health Facilities (40%). See Clarkson and Fixler (1987, Table IV-1, pp. 172-75.

Correspondence: This census category includes a wide collection of different services. The ICMA category is also broad, but the precise overlap is unknown. It is assumed that the coverage of the ICMA and the census categories is similar.[4]

The research categories are used as proxies for the whole census category by assuming that savings rates of these services are representative of the category. Clarkson and Fixler (1987) also make this assumption.

Of health services expenditures, 97% are current operating expenses. Cost-savings estimates are based solely on the operating cost, although potential rates of cost savings in construction may be higher (see discussion of housing construction).

Census Expenditure Category, Census Definition, ICMA Category or Categories, Research Categories, and Discussion of the Correspondence Among Categories from Different Sources

HIGHWAYS:

Census Definition: Construction, maintenance, and operation of highways, streets, and related structures, including toll highways, bridges, tunnels, ferries, street lighting, and snow and ice removal. However, highway policing and traffic control are classed under Police Protection.

ICMA categories: Street Repairs, Snow Plowing, Traffic Signal Installation and Maintenance, and Street Light Operation.

Research category (base): Highways.[5] See Table 3.2, service category 14.

Research category (high): Street Repair (50%), Road and Street Operation, Maintenance and Repair (50%), Traffic Signal Maintenance and Installation (40%), Streetlight Operation (25%). See Clarkson and Fixler (1987, Table IV-1, pp. 172-75.

Correspondence: The match among categories is incomplete. The research categories represent a subset of the services in the census category and the ICMA categories. It is assumed that the rate of in-house production of the services surveyed by the ICMA is similar to that for all highways programs as well as that the savings rates in the surveyed services are representative of savings rates in other highway services. Stevens (1984) found cost savings of 36% for traffic signal maintenance and 49% for asphalt overlay. To be conservative, the lower figure is used in calculating the base cost savings. Within the group of services covered by Clarkson and Fixler, the cost-savings estimates are all between 40% and 50%, with the street repairs estimate being 50%.

Research categories include both operating and capital outlays. Current operations constitute 46% of total census expenditures on highways. The cost-savings estimates are based solely on the operating cost portion of the census total which are believed to be conservative (see housing construction).

Census Expenditure Category, Census Definition, ICMA Category or Categories, Research Categories, and Discussion of the Correspondence Among Categories from Different Sources

HOSPITALS:

Census Definition: Financing, construction, acquisition, maintenance or operation of hospital facilities, provision of hospital care, and support of public or private hospitals.

ICMA category: Operation and Maintenance of Hospitals.

Research category (base): Hospitals. See Table 3.2, service category 15.

Research category (high): Operation and Management of Hospitals (55%). See Clarkson and Fixler (1987, Table IV-1, pp. 172-75.

Correspondence: The correspondence among categories is good except that the ICMA and research categories do not include construction or purchases of hospitals. Operations constitutes 94% of total census expenditures. Evidence about the effects of increased competition on construction costs (see housing) suggests that cost savings could be expected from the capital outlay portion of airport expenditures. However, to be conservative, cost-savings estimates are based solely on the operating cost portion of the census category total.

Census Expenditure Category, Census Definition, ICMA Category or Categories, Research Categories, and Discussion of the Correspondence Among Categories from Different Sources

HOUSING AND COMMUNITY DEVELOPMENT:

Census Definition: Construction and operation of housing and redevelopment projects, and other activities to promote or aid housing and community development.

ICMA category: Operation and Maintenance of Public and Elderly Housing.

Research category (base): Housing and Community Development. See Table 3.2, service category 16.

Research category (high): Housing.   See the President's Commission on Privatization (1988) in Table 3.2, service category 16.

Correspondence: The match of services is good except that the ICMA category does not include construction. In calculating the proportion of total expenditures on public housing that are produced in-house, it is assumed that contracting and other competitive approaches are used as often in construction as in operations.[6] Current operations represent 70% of total census expenditures in the category, however, since the research categories include capital construction (actual construction expenditures or consideration of construction costs through depreciation), cost savings are based on total expenditures.

Comment: The President's Commission provides comparisons of cost savings from several different approaches to providing equivalent housing assistance. The high estimate involves allowing landlords to individually compete for subsidies by accepting tenants who receive housing grants from the government.

Census Expenditure Category, Census Definition, ICMA Category or Categories, Research Categories, and Discussion of the Correspondence Among Categories from Different Sources

LIBRARIES:

Census Definition: Establishment and operation of public libraries and support of privately operated libraries (excludes those operated as part of a school system, primarily for the benefit of students and teachers, and law libraries).

ICMA category: Operation of public libraries.

Research category (base): Libraries.   See Table 3.2, service category 21.

Research category (high): Operation of Libraries (35%).   See Clarkson and Fixler (1987, Table IV-1, pp. 172-75.

Correspondence: The correspondence among the definitions of this service appears to be good, although the census category includes expenditures for establishing libraries as well as operating them. Operating expenditures account for 88% of total library expenditures according to the census. To be conservative, cost-savings estimates are based solely on the operating cost portion of libraries (see housing construction).

Comment: Libraries, like many other government services, charge some user fees (e.g., fines for overdue books) and accept donations. Because these revenues pay some of libraries' costs, government expenditures on these services are sometimes termed subsidies. In general, however, the fact that government expenditures are termed subsidies does not mean that libraries operate as independent entities. Even though these independent sources of income may confer a measure of autonomy, libraries are operated as government departments. Roughly 90% of the ICMA's survey respondents (among those with any library expenditures) operate libraries in-house or cooperate with other governments in operating libraries. See Valente and Manchester (1984).

Census Expenditure Category, Census Definition, ICMA Category or Categories, Research Categories, and Discussion of the Correspondence Among Categories from Different Sources

PARKING FACILITIES:

Census Definition: Construction, purchase, maintenance, and operation of public use parking lots, garages, parking meters, and other distinctive parking facilities on a commercial basis.

ICMA categories: Parking Lot and Garage Operation and Maintenance and Parking Meter Maintenance and Collections.

Research category (base): Parking. See Table 3.2, service category 26.

Research category (high): Parking Lot and Garage Operation (31%), Meter Maintenance and Installation (33%). See Clarkson and Fixler (1987, Table IV-1, pp. 172-75.

Correspondence: The base research category source relates to parking meter and garage enforcement activities, a subset of the census category. The savings rate from this subset of services is used as a proxy for the category on the assumption that it is representative of the services within the census category. Clarkson and Fixler (1987) use a similar assumption in reporting similar savings rates (low estimates of 14% and 15%) for both services within this census category.

The census category includes construction expenditures as well as operating expenditures. Operating expenditures constitute 61% of total expenditures reported in the census. Evidence about the effects of increased competition on construction costs (see housing) suggests that cost savings could be expected from the capital outlay portion of parking expenditures. However, to be conservative, cost-savings estimates are based solely on the operating cost portion.

Census Expenditure Category, Census Definition, ICMA Category or Categories, Research Categories, and Discussion of the Correspondence Among Categories from Different Sources

PARKS AND RECREATION:

Census Definition: Provision and support of recreational and cultural-scientific facilities and activities including golf courses, playfields, playgrounds, public beaches, swimming pools, tennis courts, parks, auditoriums, stadiums, auto camps, recreation piers, marinas, botanical garden galleries, museums, and zoos. Also includes building and operation of convention centers and exhibition halls.

ICMA categories: Recreation Services, Operation and Maintenance of Recreation Facilities, Park Landscape Maintenance, Operation of Convention Centers, Operation of Cultural Arts Programs, Operation of Museums.

Research category (base): Parks and Recreation. See Table 3.2, service category 27.

Research category (high): Recreation Services (52%), Recreation Facilities Operation and Management (52%), Park Landscaping and Maintenance (28%), Cultural Arts Operations (28%), Auditorium Operations (35%), Operation of Museums (35%). See Clarkson and Fixler (1987, Table IV-1, pp. 172-75.

Correspondence: The match among services is incomplete, but includes a variety of services from the overall census category. The Stevens (1984) estimate for park landscaping and maintenance is used as the proxy. Stevens provides a superior evaluation that controls for quality and other factors and evidence suggests that savings rates for landscaping activities are lower than for recreation activities and hence using the landscaping cost-savings rate is a conservative assumption.[7] Further, the cost-savings rate from Stevens is also similar to the facilities construction cost-savings estimate report by Savas (1987). Since the research categories include both operating (74%) and construction cost (26%), so do the cost-savings estimates.

Census Expenditure Category, Census Definition, ICMA Category or Categories, Research Categories, and Discussion of the Correspondence Among Categories from Different Sources

PUBLIC WELFARE:

Census Definition: Support of and assistance to needy persons contingent on their need.[8] Expenditures under this heading include Cash Assistance paid directly to needy persons under the categorical programs (e.g., Aid to Families with Dependent Children)[9] and under any other welfare programs; Vendor Payments made directly to private purveyors of medical care, burials, and other commodities and services provided under welfare programs, and provision and operation by the government of Welfare Institutions. Other Public Welfare includes payment to other governments for welfare purposes, amounts for administration, support of private welfare agencies, and other public welfare services.[10]

ICMA category: Child Welfare Programs.

Research category (base): Public Welfare. See Table 3.2, service category 33.

Research category (high): Child Welfare Program Management. See Clarkson and Fixler (1987, Table IV-1, pp. 172-75.

Correspondence: The correspondence among categories appears to be good with respect to program management of the major child welfare programs, a major subset of welfare programs[11] and is used as a proxy for welfare services generally.

In addition to operating expenditures, the census category also includes direct transfers to needy persons as well as construction funding. Since increasing competition in management of welfare programs will have no effect on direct transfer payments, these payments should be excluded in the cost-savings calculations. Current operating expenditures, which exclude direct transfers and capital outlays, comprise 73% of total census expenditures. The cost-savings estimates are based exclusively on operating costs.

Census Expenditure Category, Census Definition, ICMA Category or Categories, Research Categories, and Discussion of the Correspondence Among Categories from Different Sources

REFUSE COLLECTION (Sanitation other than Sewerage):

Census Definition: Street Cleaning, solid waste collection and disposal, and provision for sanitary landfills.

ICMA categories: Residential Solid Waste Collection, Commercial Solid Waste Collection, Solid Waste Disposal, and Street Cleaning.

Research category (base): Refuse Collection, Street Cleaning. See Table 3.2, service categories 35 and 41.

Research category (high): Residential Refuse. See Savas (1974) in Table 3.2, service category 35.[12]

Correspondence: The match among the ICMA and census categories appears to be good. The base research category includes collection of refuse and street cleaning but does not include disposal of refuse. The included categories are used as proxies for the whole category on the assumption that they are representative of the category. The savings rate for refuse collection is assumed to be representative of all the component services. This is a conservative assumption since Stevens' cost-savings rate estimate for street cleaning is higher. Clarkson and Fixler (1987) utilize the assumption that cost-savings rates are similar (30%) for different refuse services in assigning the same savings rate to all of the services within the census category except street sweeping (39%).

The research categories include consideration of capital expenditures (16% of total costs), hence, the cost-savings calculations are based on total expenditures in the census category.

Census Expenditure Category, Census Definition, ICMA Category or Categories, Research Categories, and Discussion of the Correspondence Among Categories from Different Sources

SEWERAGE (Wastewater Treatment):

Census Definition: Provision of sanitary and storm sewers and sewage disposal facilities and services, and payments to other governments for such purposes.

ICMA categories: Utility Meter Reading and Utility Billing. Independent evidence indicates similar rates of in-house production for utility operations and capital projects.

Research category (base): Sewerage/ Wastewater Treatment. See Table 3.2, service category 38.

Research category (high): Wastewater Treatment. See Moore (1987) in Table 3.2, service category 38).

Correspondence: The census and research categories appear to match well. The ICMA category, however, covers only a portion of sewerage service operations and does not cover capital/construction projects. Independent evidence indicates that both capital projects and operations are conducted in-house in approximately the same proportion.[13] Therefore, the use of the ICMA ratio for meter reading and billing should be a reasonable proxy for the ratio between in-house and other types of production operations in the category.

Since the research categories include consideration of both operating and capital outlays, the cost-savings calculation are based on total costs in the category. Operations account for 51% of total outlays.

Census Expenditure Category, Census Definition, ICMA Category or Categories, Research Categories, and Discussion of the Correspondence Among Categories from Different Sources

TRANSIT:

Census Definition: Payments in support of subway, bus, surface rail, street railroad, and other passenger transportation systems, including public support of private transportation utilities or railroads, and intergovernmental subsidy payments. Excludes amounts paid by a parent government to its dependent transit utility.

ICMA categories: Operation and Maintenance of Bus Systems and Operation and Maintenance of Paratransit Systems.

Research category (base): Bus Service. See Table 3.2, service category 6.

Research category (high): Bus Service. See Walters (1987) in Table 3.2, service category 6.

Correspondence: The match among categories is incomplete. The ICMA and research categories deal primarily with the operation of buses while the census category includes other transit modes. The bus cost-savings rate is assumed to be representative of cost-savings rates for all varieties of public transit.[14]

Another difficulty arises because the census figures are limited to transit subsidies while the research categories concern total costs of bus operations, some of which are paid by fares and some by government subsidies. The cost-savings calculations assume that the total cost-savings rates are equal to the subsidy savings rates. This is a conservative assumption since the subsidy savings rates are higher than the cost-savings rates whenever fares or other sources of income are greater than zero.[15]

The research category includes consideration of capital outlays as well as operating expenditures, hence the cost saving estimates are based on total expenditures in the category.

Census Expenditure Category, Census Definition, ICMA Category or Categories, Research Categories, and Discussion of the Correspondence Among Categories from Different Sources

UTILITY EXPENDITURES:

Census Definition: Expenditures for construction of utility facilities or equipment, for production and distribution of utility commodities and services (except those furnished to the parent government), and for interest on debt. Does not include expenditure in connection with administration of debt and investments (treated as general expenditure) and the cost of providing service to the parent government. A utility means a government owned and operated water supply, electric light and power, gas supply, or *transit system*.[16] Also see Transit Subsidies.

ICMA categories: Operation and Maintenance of Bus Systems and Operation and Maintenance of Paratransit Systems, Utility Meter Reading, and Utility Billing.

Research categories (base): Bus Service, and Electric and Water Utilities. See Table 3.2, categories 6, 10, and 43.

Research category (high): Bus Transit (60%), Rail Transit (60%), Electric Utility (25%), Gas Utility (25%), Water Utility (25%), Utility Meter Reading (25%), Utility Billing (25%). See Clarkson and Fixler (1987, Table IV-1, pp. 172-75.

Correspondence: The match between categories is incomplete, since the census category is broader than the others. The base cost-savings estimates from electric and water utilities (0%) are used on the assumption that they are representative. This is a conservative assumption since rate for the bus component of utilities is 28%.

The ICMA category is a subset of the categories from the other data sources. The in-house expenditures calculation is based on the assumption that the average cost-savings rates from competitivization for bus service, utility billing, and meter reading are similar or greater than the rates for other aspects of utility operations. Both operating (64%) and capital costs (36%) are included in the cost-savings estimates.

NOTES

1. Data on state and local government expenditures and the proportion of these expenditures devoted to operating expenses, capital projects, and direct income transfers are taken from the annual survey of governments for 1986-87 (U.S. Department of Commerce, 1988).

2. Stocker (1980) found a higher cost savings rate of 50% with respect to assessments.

3. See Hanke (1985a) for some limited evidence on cost savings on contracted ambulance services.

Sewerage treatment operations are classified under Sewerage.

4. In considering this assumption, it should be recalled that cities and counties regularly have to complete census forms, so it does not seem unreasonable to suppose that governments would utilize census definitions in responding to the ICMA survey, especially given that the ICMA study was sponsored, in part by the federal government (Department of Housing and Urban Development).

5. Includes traffic signal maintenance and repairs.

6. David (1988) indicates that private competitive production of services formerly produced by local governments has developed in both operations and capital projects.

7. Clarkson (1987) also reports savings rates for recreational services that are greater (nearly twice as high) as those for landscaping services.

8. Excludes pensions to former employees and other benefits not contingent on need.

9. Other programs in this category include Old Age Assistance, Aid to the Blind, and Aid to the Disabled.

10. Health and hospital services provided directly by the government through its own hospitals and health agencies, and any payments to other government for such purposes are classed under those functional headings rather than here.

11. *1988 World Almanac*, New York: Scripps Howard, 1987, p. 543.

12. Cost savings estimates in additional refuse collection services include Commercial Solid Waste Collection (30%), Solid Waste Disposal (30%), and Street/Parking Lot Cleaning (39%). See Clarkson and Fixler (1987, Table IV-1, pp. 172-75.

13. Approximately 70% of respondents in a recent Touche Ross survey of privatization in local government did not use private contracting in constructing sewerage facilities (capital projects) during the five years from 1982 to 1987. The ICMA survey found that in-house production was used exclusively in a similar proportion of jurisdictions responsible for utility billing (62%) and in a similar proportion of the jurisdictions for utility meter reading (64%). (Personal communication with Irwin T. David, Touche Ross

(1988), and David (1988, Chapter 5, pp. 43-55.) The lower in-house ratios are used in the cost-savings calculations. This has the effect of reducing the estimates of in-house expenditures and cost savings and therefore is a conservative assumption.

14. Bus systems are much more common than the other forms of transportation, which typically require very high route densities to be economically viable. Clarkson assigns similar cost savings rates to both rail and bus service categories. See utilities.

15. For example, if 50% of costs are currently paid by a government subsidy, and then increased competition reduces overall costs by 20%, the government subsidy could be reduced by 40%, all else remaining equal.

It is also assumed that subsidies are primarily allocated to transit operations that are not currently subject of competitive contracting or other forms of competition.

16. Government revenue, expenditure, and debt relating to utility facilities leased to other governments or persons, and other commercial type activities of government, such as port facilities, airports, housing project, radio stations, steam plants, ferries, and abattoirs (slaughterhouses), are classified as governmental activities.

Bibliography

Adams, W. 1977. "The Steel Industry." In W. Adams, ed., *The Structure of American Industry*, 86-129. 5th ed. New York: Macmillan.

Adie, D. 1989. *Monopoly Mail: Privatizing the United States Postal Service*. New Brunswick, New Jersey: Transaction Publishers.

_____. 1987. "Deregulating, Divesting, and Privatizing the United States Postal System." Reason Foundation Issue Paper (July 16).

_____. 1977. *An Evaluation of Postal Service Wage Rates*. Washington, D.C.: American Enterprise Institute.

Ahlbrandt, R. 1974. "Implications of Contracting for Public Service." *Urban Affairs Quarterly* 9:337-58.

_____. 1973. "Efficiency in the Provision of Fire Services." *Public Choice* 16:1-15.

Aiken, M., and J. Hage. 1971. "Organizational Interdependence and Intra-Organizational Structure." In Maurer, J., ed., *Readings in Organizational Theory: Open Systems Approaches*, 300-324. New York: Random House.

Alchian, A. 1965. "The Basis of Some Recent Advances in the Theory of Management of the Firm." *Journal of Industrial Economics* 14(1):30-41 (November).

Alchian, A., and H. Demsetz. 1973. "The Property Rights Paradigm." *Journal of Economic History* 33:16-27 (March).

_____. 1972. "Production, Information Costs, and Economic Organization." *American Economic Review* 62:777-95.

Alger, D. 1986. *Investigating Oligopolies within the Laboratory*. Washington, D.C.: U.S. Federal Trade Commission.

Alwin, L. 1987. *Competitive Cost Review Cost Analysis Guide*. Austin, Texas: Office of the State Auditor.

American Federation of State, County, and Municipal Employees. 1988. *The Privatization/Contracting Out Debate*. Washington, D.C.: AFSCME.

_____. 1983. *Passing the Bucks: Contracting Out of Public Services.* Washington, D.C.: AFSCME.

_____. "Government for Sale." Washington, D.C.: AFSCME, undated pamphlet.

Armington, R., and W. Ellis, eds. 1984. *This Way Up: The Local Officials' Handbook for Privatization and Contracting Out.* Lake Bluff, Ill.: Regnery Gateway Inc.

Arrow, K. 1974. *Limits of Organization.* New York: Norton.

Asher, M., and J. Popkin. 1984. "The Effect of Gender and Race Differentials on Public-Private Wage Comparisons: A Study of Postal Workers." *Industrial and Labor Relations Review* 38(1):16-25 (October).

Atkinson, S., and R. Halvorsen. 1986. "The Relative Efficiency of Public And Private Firms in a Regulated Environment: The Case of U.S. Electric Utilities." *Journal of Public Economics* 20:281-94 (April).

Auerbach, S. 1991. "Around the Globe, the Sale of the Century: Sweeping Privatization Sends State Industries to the Auction Block - and a Philosophy to the Scrap Heap." *Washington Post* (November 17):H1,H9.

Bacon, K. 1990. "Use of Free-Enterprise Philosophy Is Urged for Reform of Public Schools." *Wall Street Journal* (June 5):A26.

Bailey, R. 1987. "Uses and Misuses of Privatization." In S. Hanke, ed. *Prospects for Privatization, Proceedings of the Academy of Political Science* 36(3):138-52.

Bandow, D. 1990. "Offering Worse Service at Higher Prices." *Washington Times* (March 2):F.

Baumol, W. 1959. *Business Behavior, Value, and Growth.* New York: Macmillan.

Baumol, W. and K. Lee. 1991. "Contestable Markets, Trade, and Development." *World Bank Research Observer* 6(1):1-17 (January).

Baumol, W., J. Panzar, and R. Willig. 1986. "On the Thoery of Perfectly Contestable Markets." In J. Stiglitz and F. Mathewson, eds., *New Developments in the Analysis of Market Structure.* Cambridge, Massachusetts: MIT Press.

_____. 1982. *Contestable Markets and the Theory of Industrial Structure.* New York: Harcourt, Brace, and Jovanovich.

Becker, E., and F. Sloan. 1985. "Hospital Ownership and Performance." *Economic Inquiry* 23:21-36.

Bellamy, J. 1981. "Two Utilities Are Better Than One." *Reason* 12 (October).

Bendick, M., Jr. 1982. "On the Efficiency of Markets Created by Government: A Review of Recent Experience with the For-Profit Privatization of Public Services." Urban Institute Project Report.

Bennett, J., and M. Johnson. 1981. *Better Government at Half the Price!* Ottawa, Il.: Caroline House Publishers, Inc.

_____. 1980. "Tax Reduction Without Sacrifice: Private Sector Production of Public Services." *Public Finance Quarterly* 8:363-96.

_____. 1979. "Public versus Private Provision of Collective Goods and Services: Garbage Collection Revisited." *Public Choice* 34:55-64.

Bennett, J., and T. DiLorenzo. 1983. "Public Employee Unions and the Privatization of "Public" Services." *Journal of Labor Research* 4(1):33-45 (Winter).

Benton, W., Jr. 1979. "Questions for Research and Development." In Wedel, K., A. Katz, and A. Weick, eds. *Social Services by Government Contract: A Policy Analysis*, 81-91. New York: Praeger.

Berle, A., and G. Means. 1932. *The Modern Corporation and Private Property*. New York: Commerce Clearing House.

Bish, R., and R. Warren. 1972. "Scale and Monopoly Problems in Urban Government Services." *Urban Affairs Quarterly* 8(1):97-122 (September).

Blair, R., and D. Kaserman. 1983. *Law and Economics of Vertical Integration and Control*. Orlando, Fl.: Harcourt, Brace, and Jovanovich.

Blankart, C. 1987. "Limits to Privatization." *European Economic Review* 31:346-51.

Blyskal, J., and M. Hodge. 1987. "Why Your Mail Is So Slow?" *New York* (November 9):43-55.

Boardman, A., and A. Vining. 1989. "Ownership and Performance in Competitive Environments: A Comparison of the Performance of Private, Mixed, and State-owned Enterprises." *Journal of Law and Economics* 32(1):1-33 (April).

Borcherding, T. 1978. "Competition, Exclusion, and the Optimal Supply of Public Goods." *Journal of Law and Economics* 21:111-32.

Borcherding, T., W. Pommerehne, and F. Schneider. 1982. "Comparing the Efficiency of Private and Public Production: The Evidence from Five Countries." *Journal of Economics* (suppl. 2):127-56.

Bos, D. 1987. "Privatization of Public Enterprises." *European Economic Review* 31:352-360.

Bovard, J. 1990. "The Slow Death of the U.S. Postal Service." In P. Ferrara, ed., *Free the Mail*, 11-30. Washington, D.C.: Cato Institute.

Brennan, G., and J. Buchanan. 1980. *The Power to Tax: Analytical Foundations of a Fiscal Constitution.* Cambridge, U.K.: Cambridge University Press.

Brenton, A., and R. Wintrobe. 1975. "The Equilibrium Size of a Budget-Maximizing Bureau: A Note on Niskanen's Theory of Bureaucracy." *Journal of Political Economy* 83:195-207 (February).

Bundesrechnungshof. 1972. "Bemerkungen des Bundesrechnungshofs zur Bundeshaushaltsrechnung (einschlieBlich Bundesvermogen-srechnung) fuer das Haushaltsjahr." *Bundestagsdrucksache* 7/2709:110-111. Cited in T. Borcherding, W. Pommerehne, and F. Schneider, "Comparing the Efficiency of Private and Public Production: The Evidence from Five Countries." *Journal of Economics* (suppl. 2):127-56.

Bundesregierung Deutschland. 1976. "Agrarbericht 1976." *Bundestagsdrucksache* (7/4680):63-65, and *Bundestagsdrucksache* (7/4681):146. Cited in T. Borcherding, W. Pommerehne, and F. Schneider, "Comparing the Efficiency of Private and Public Production: The Evidence from Five Countries." *Journal of Economics* (suppl. 2):127-56.

Burton, J. 1987. "Privatization: The Thatcher Case." *Managerial and Decision Economics* 8:21-29.

Butler, S., ed. 1985. *The Privatization Option.* Heritage Foundation Lectures #42. Washington, D.C.: Heritage Foundation.

Campbell, A. 1988. "Private Delivery of Public Services: Sorting Out the Policy and Management Issues." *Public Management* 68(12):3-5 (December).

Canada, Auditor General of, Report of 1985. 1985. Ottawa: Office of the Auditor General, Section 13.

Caponiti, F., and E. Booher. 1986. "An Enforcement Alternative." *The Parking Professional* (November):16-22.

Carlson, E. 1991. "Privatization Lets Small Firms Manage Everything from Libraries to Golf Courses." *Wall Street Journal* (April 2):B1,B2.

Caves, D., and L. Christensen. 1980. "The Relative Efficiency of Public and Private Firms in a Competitive Environment: The Case of Canadian Railroads." *Journal of Political Economy* 88:958-76.

Chapman, J. 1981. "Fees and Charges, Rule Use, and Land Development in Post Proposition 13 California." *Urban Interest* 3:13-21 (Spring).

Clarkson, K. 1989. "Privatization and Economic Performance in Britain: A Comment." *Carnegie-Rochester Conference Series on Public Policy* 31:345-52.

Clarkson, K., and P. Fixler, Jr. 1987. *The Role of Privatization in Florida's Growth*. Tallahassee, Fl.: Florida Chamber of Commerce Foundation.

_____. 1972. "Some Implications of Property Rights in Hospital Management." *Journal of Law and Economics* 15:363-84.

Coase, R. 1988a. "The Firm, the Market, and the Law." In R. Coase, *The Firm, The Market, and the Law*, 1-31, Chicago: University of Chicago Press.

_____. 1988b. "The Nature of the Firm: Meaning." *Journal of Law, Economics, and Organization* 4(1):19-32 (Spring).

_____. 1937. "The Nature of the Firm." *Economica* 4:386-405 (November).

Collins, J., and B. Downes. 1977. "The Effect of Size on the Provision of Public Services: The Case of Solid Waste Collection in Smaller Cities." *Urban Affairs Quarterly* 12:333-34.

Conover, H. 1977. *Grounds Maintenance Handbook*, 3rd. ed. New York: McGraw-Hill. Cited in B. Stevens, *Delivering Municipal Services Efficiently: A Comparison of Municipal and Private Service Delivery*. Washington, D.C.: U.S. Department of Housing and Urban Development.

Courant, P., E. Gramlich, and D. Rubenfeld. 1980. "Why Voters Support Tax Limitation Amendments: The Michigan Case." *National Tax Journal* 33:1-20.

Crain, W., and A. Zardkoohi. 1978. "A Test of the Property Rights Theory of the Firm: Water Utilities in the United States." *Journal of Law and Economics* 21:395-408.

Current Municipal Problems staff. 1987. "Privatized Wastewater Facility in Auburn." *Current Municipal Problems* 14(1):61-66.

David, I. 1988. "Privatization in America." In *Municipal Year Book, 1988*, 43-55. Washington D.C., International City Management Association.

_____. 1987. *Privatization in America*. Washington, D.C.: Touche Ross.

Davies, D. 1982. "Property Rights and Economic Behavior in Private and Government Enterprises: The Case of Australia's Banking System." *Research in Law and Economics* 3:111-42.

_____. 1977. "Property Rights and Economic Efficiency: The Australian Airlines Revisited." *Journal of Law and Economics* 20:223-26.

_____. 1971. "The Efficiency of Public versus Private Firms: The Case of Australia's Two Airlines." *Journal of Law and Economics* 14:149-65.

Deacon, R. 1979. "The Expenditure Effects of Alternative Public Supply Institutions." *Public Choice* 34(3-4):381-97.

DeHoog, R. 1981. *Political and Economic Approaches to Government 'Contracting Out': A Study of Human Services Contracting in the State of Michigan.* Ph.D. diss., Michigan State University.

Demsetz, H. 1968. "Why Regulate Utilities?" *Journal of Law and Economics* 11:55-66 (April).

DeVaney, A. 1976. "Uncertainty, Waiting Time, and Capacity Utilization: A Stochastic Theory of Product Quality." *Journal of Political Economy* 84(3):523-41 (June).

Domberger, S., and J. Piggott. 1986. "Privatization Policies and Public Enterprise: A Survey." *Economic Record* 62:145-62 (June).

Downs, A. 1967. *Inside Bureaucracy.* Boston: Little, Brown.

Downs, G., and P. Larkey. 1986. *The Search for Government Efficiency: From Hubris to Helplessness.* New York: Random House.

_____. 1981. "Fiscal Reform and Government Efficiency: Hanging Tough." *Policy Sciences* 13:381-96.

Dudek and Co. 1988. *Privatization and Public Employees: The Impact of City and County Contracting Out on Government Workers.* Washington, D.C.: National Commission for Employment Policy.

Edwards, F., and B. Stevens. 1979. "Relative Efficiency of Alternative Institutional Arrangements for Collecting Refuse: Collective Action vs. the Free Market." New York: Columbia University. Mimeo.

Feigenbaum, S., and R. Teeples. 1982. "Public Versus Private Water Delivery: A Hedonic Cost Approach." Claremont, California: Claremont Graduate School (June). Cited in E. Savas, *Privatization: The Key to Better Government*, 149-150. Chatham, New Jersey: Chatham House Publishers, Inc.

Feldman, R., C. Berrocal, and H. Sharfsten. 1987. "Public Finance Through Privatization: Providing Infrastructure for the Future." *Stetson Law Review* 16:705-34.

Ferris, J., and E. Graddy. 1986. "Contracting Out: For What? With Whom?" *Public Administration Review* 46(4):332-444 (July/August).

Finsinger, J. 1981. "Competition, Ownership and Control in Markets with Imperfect Information: The Case of the German Liability and Life Insurance Markets." Berlin: International Institute of Management, Berlin. Mimeo. Cited in T. Borcherding, W. Pommerehne, and F. Schneider, "Comparing the Efficiency of Private and Public Production: The Evidence from Five Countries." *Journal of Economics* (suppl. 2):127-56.

Fischer-Menshausen, H. 1975. "Entlastung des Staates durch Privatisierung von Aufgaben." *Wirtschaftsdienst* 55:545-52. Cited in T. Borcherding, W. Pommerehne, and F. Schneider, "Comparing the

Efficiency of Private and Public Production in Five Countries." *Journal of Economics* (suppl. 2):127-56.

Fisk, D., H. Kiesling, and T. Muller. 1978. *Private Provision of Public Services: An Overview.* Washington, D.C.: Urban Institute.

Fixler, P., Jr., and R. Poole. 1987. "Status of State and Local Privatization." in S. Hanke, ed., *Prospects for Privatization, Proceedings of the Academy of Political Science* 36(3):164-78.

Forbes, K., and E. Zampelli. 1989. "Is Leviathan a Mythical Beast?" *American Economic Review* 79(3):568-77 (June).

Frech, H. 1979. "Mutual and Other Nonprofit Health Insurance Firms: Comparative Performance in a Natural Experiment." *Research in Law and Economics* (Supplement to vol. 1):61-73.

_____. 1976. "The Property Rights Theory of the Firm: Empirical Results from a Natural Experiment." *Journal of Political Economy* 84:143-52.

Frey, B., and W. Pommerehne. 1982. "How Powerful Are Public Bureaucrats as Voters?" *Public Choice* 38(3):253-62.

Frug, J. 1987. "The Choice Between Privatization and Publicazation." *Current Municipal Problems* 14(1):20-26.

Gallick, E. 1984. *Exclusive Dealing and Vertical Integration: The Efficiency of Contracts in the Tuna Industry.* Washington, D.C.: Federal Trade Commission.

Gardels, N. 1989. "Perestroika Goes South: Auctioning Off the National Patrimony." *New York Times* (November 12):2F.

Gillette, C., and T. Hopkins. 1987. "Federal User Fees: A Legal and Economic Analysis." *Boston University Law Review* 67(5):795-874 (November).

Goldberg, V. 1976. "Regulation and Administered Contracts." *Bell Journal of Economics* 7:426-48 (August).

Goldman, H., and S. Mokuvos. 1984. *The Privatization Book.* New York: Arthur Young and Company.

Goodsell, C. 1983. *The Case For Bureaucracy: A Public Administration Polemic.* Chatham, New Jersey: Chatham House Publishers, Inc..

Gordon, B. 1984. *Contracting-Out for Support Services by U.S. Counties and Municipalities: The Political Aspects.* Ph.D. diss., University of Maryland, College Park.

Grannemann, T, R. Brown, and M. Pauly. 1986. "Estimating Hospital Costs: A Multiple Output Analysis." *Journal of Health Economics* 5:107-27.

Grant, J., and D. Bast. 1987. "Corrections and the Private Sector: A Guide for Public Officials." Chicago: Heartland Institute (May).

Green, W. 1986. "Competition and Monopoly in the Mails." *Journal of the Institute for Socioeconomic Studies* 11(1):74-85 (Summer).

Greer, D. 1984. *Industrial Organization and Public Policy*. New York: Macmillan.

Hamburger Senat. 1974. *AbschluBbericht des Beauftragten zur Gebaudereinigung*. Hamburg: Hamburger Senat. Cited in T. Borcherding, W. Pommerehne, and F. Schneider, "Comparing the Efficiency of Private and Public Production: The Evidence from Five Countries." *Journal of Economics* (suppl. 2):127-56.

Hanke, S. 1985a. "The Literature on Privatization." In S. Butler, ed., *The Privatization Option*, 83-97. Washington, D.C.: The Heritage Foundation.

_____. 1985b. "The Theory of Privatization." In S. Butler, ed., *The Privatization Option*, 1-14. Washington, D.C.: The Heritage Foundation.

_____, ed. 1987. *Prospects for Privatization, Proceedings of the Academy of Political Science* 36(3).

Harney, D. 1986. "A Purchasing Agent's View of Privatization." *Public Management* 68(12):16-18 (December).

Hart, O. 1983. "The Market Mechanism as an Incentive Scheme." *Bell Journal of Economics* 14(2):366-82 (Autumn).

Hatry, H. 1983. *A Review of Private Approaches for Delivery of Public Services*. Washington, D.C.: Urban Institute.

Hellman, R. 1972. *Government Competition in the Electric Utility Industry*. New York: Praeger.

Hilke, J. 1986. "The Impact of Volunteer Firefighters on Local Government Spending and Taxation." *Municipal Finance Journal* 7(1):33-44 (Winter).

Hilke, J., and M. Vita. 1989. Testimony on "Comments of the Staff of the Bureau of Economics of the Federal Trade Commission." In *Monopoly Theory Inquiry, Docket RM89-4*, 120-37,356-90 Washington, D.C.: United States of American Postal Rate Commission.

Hinds, M. 1991. "Cash-Strapped Cities Turn to Companies to Do What Government Once Did." *New York Times* (May 14):A12.

Hirsch, W. 1965. "Cost Functions of Urban Government Services: Refuse Collection." *Review of Economics and Statistics* 47:87-92. Cited in T. Borcherding, W. Pommerehne, and F. Schneider, "Comparing the Efficiency of Private and Public Production: The Evidence from Five Countries." *Journal of Economics* (suppl. 2):127-56.

Hodge, S. 1986. "Privatizing Fire Protection: A Case Study." Chicago: Heartland Institute.

Holmes, P. 1985. "Taking Services Private." *Nation's Business* (August):20-25.

Houlden, P., and S. Balkin. 1985. "Quality and Cost Comparisons of Private Bare Indigent Defense Systems: Contract vs. Ordered Assigned Counsel." *Journal of Criminal Law and Criminology* 76(1):176-200.

Hsiao, W. 1978. "Public Versus Private Administration of Health Insurance: A Study in Relative Economic Efficiency." *Inquiry* 15:379-87 (December).

Humphrey, C. 1990. *Privatization in Bangladesh: Economic Transition in a Poor Country.* Boulder, Colorado: Westview Press.

Ippolito, P. 1986. "Consumer Protection Economics: A Selective Survey." In P. Ippolito and D. Scheffman, eds., *Empirical Approaches to Consumer Protection Economics*, 1-37. Washington, D.C.: Federal Trade Commission.

Ippolito, P., and D. Scheffman, eds. 1986. *Empirical Approaches to Consumer Protection Economics.* Washington, D.C.: Federal Trade Commission.

Judis, J. 1988. "Mission Impossible: The Postal Service Struggles with Old Problems, New Competition -- and the Public." *New York Times Magazine* (September 25):31-33, 50-54.

Kaiser, C. 1977. "Custodial Services in Schools Termed Wasteful by Goldin." *New York Times* (January):45.

_____. 1976. "Private Towaways." *New York Times* (September 4).

Kamm, T. 1991. "Going Private: South Americans Push Sales of State Assests in Swing to Capitalism." *Wall Street Journal* (July 9):A1,A4.

Kelley, J. 1984. *Costing Government Services: A Guide for Decision Making.* Washington, D.C.: Government Finance Officers' Association.

Kemper, P., and J. Quigley. 1976. *The Economics of Refuse Collection.* Cambridge, Mass.: Ballinger.

Kennedy, K., and R. Mehr. 1977. "A Case Study in Private versus Public Enterprise: The Manitoba Experience with Automobile Insurance." *Journal of Risk and Insurance* 4:595-621.

King, T. 1986. *How to Cut Government Spending and Improve Public Services in Illinois.* Chicago: Heartland Institute.

Kitchen, H. 1976. "A Statistical Estimation of an Operating Cost Function for Municipal Refuse Collection." *Public Finance Quarterly* 4:56-76.

Klein, B., R. Crawford, and A. Alchien. 1978. "Vertical Integration, Appropriable Rents, and the Competitive Contracting Process." *Journal of Law and Economics* 21:297-326 (October).

Klein, B., and K. Leffler. 1981. "The Role of Market Forces in Assuring Contractual Performance." *Journal of Political Economy* 89:615-41 (August).

Koo, A. 1990 "The Contract Responsibility System: Transition from a Planned to a Market Economy." *Economic Development and Cultural Change* 38(4):787-820 (July).

Kristensen, O. 1983. "Public Versus Private Provision of Governmental Services: The Case of Danish Fire Protection Services." *Urban Studies* 20:1-9.

Kwoka, J. 1989. "International Joint Venture: General Motors and Toyota." In J. Kwoka and L. White, eds., *The Antitrust Revolution*, 46-79. Glenview, Ill.: Scott, Foresmann.

Lampkin, L. 1988. "Testimony before the President's Commission on Privatization." Washington, D.C.: AFSCME (January 7).

Leibenstein, H. 1976. *Beyond Economic Man*. Cambridge, Mass.: Harvard University Press.

Lentz, B. 1981. "Political and Economic Determinants of County Government Pay." *Public Choice* 36:253-71 (Spring).

Lewis, D., N. Maxwell, and V. Sahgal. 1988. "Methodology for Auditing Cost-Recoverable Programs: Theory and Practice." *International Journal of Government Auditing* (January):11-15,19.

Lindsay, C. 1976. "A Theory of Government Enterprise." *Journal of Political Economy* 84(2):1061-77.

_____. 1975. *Veterans Administration Hospitals*. Washington, D.C.: American Enterprise Institute.

Litvan, L., and L. Cauley. 1988. "Private Mail Gives Variety of Services." *Washington Times* (April 1):C1-C3.

Lourie, N. 1979. "Purchase of Service Contracting: Issues Confronting the Government Sponsored Agency." In K. Wedel, A. Katz, and A. Weick, eds., *Social Services by Government Contract: A Policy Analysis,* 18-29. New York: Praeger.

Lynch, M., R. Miller, C. Plott, and R. Porter. 1986. "Product Quality, Consumer Information, and 'Lemons' in Experimental Markets." In P. Ippolito and D. Scheffman, eds., *Empirical Approaches to Consumer Protection Economics*, 251-306. Washington, D.C.: Federal Trade Commission.

MacAvoy, P., and G. McIsaac. 1987. "The Management of Federally Sponsored Corporations." Paper delivered at the University of Rochester conference on "Privatization in Britain and North America: Theory, Evidence, and Implementation." Washington, D.C. (November 6).

McDavid, J., and E. Butler. 1984. *Fire Services in Canadian Municipalities*. Victoria, B.C., Canada: University of Victoria. Cited in E. Savas, *Privatization: The Key to Better Government*. Chatham, New Jersey: Chatham House.

Mann, P., and J. Mikesell. 1976. "Ownership and Water Systems Operations." *Water Resources Bulletin* 12:995-1004.

Marlin, J. 1984. *Contracting Municipal Services: A Guide for Purchase from the Private Sector.* New York: Wiley and Sons.

Martin, D. 1986. "A Construction Alternative." *The Parking Professional* (November):22-24.

Maass, P. 1991. "Flood of Foreign Investment Capitalizes on New Hungary." *Washington Post* (November 10):H1,H5.

Matlack, C. 1988. "No Pickup, No Delivery." *National Journal* (June 4):1480-84.

McChesney, F. 1986. "Government Prohibitions on Volunteer Fire Fighting in Nineteenth-Century America: A Property Rights Perspective." *Journal of Legal Studies* 15:69-92 (January).

McEntee, G. 1985. "City Services: Can Free Enterprise Outperform the Public Sector?" *Business & Society Review* 55:43-47 (Fall).

McKean, R. 1972. "Property Rights Within Government and Devises to Increase Government Efficiency." *Southern Economic Journal* 39(2):177-86.

Mehay, S. 1979. "Intergovernmental Contracting for Municipal Police Services: An Empirical Analysis." *Land Economics* 55(1):59-72 (February).

Mehay, S., and R. Gonzalez. 1985. "Economic Incentives Under Contract Supply of Local Government Services." *Public Choice* 46:79-86.

Meyer, R. 1975. "Publicly Owned versus Privately Owned Utilities: A Policy Choice." *Review of Economics and Statistics* 57:391-99.

Migue, J., and G. Belanger. 1974. "Toward a General Theory of Managerial Discretion." *Public Choice* 17:27-43 (Spring).

Millward, R. 1982. "The Comparative Performance of Public and Private Ownership." In Roll, Lord of Ipsden, ed., *The Mixed Economy* 58-93. London: Macmillan.

Monsen, R., and A. Downes. 1965. "A Theory of Large Managerial Firms." *Journal of Political Economy* 73(3):221-36 (June).

Moore, S. 1988. "Privatization in America's Cities: Lessons for Washington, Part I." Heritage Foundation Backgrounder #652 (May 31).

_____. 1987. "Contracting Out: A Painless Alternative to the Budget Cutter's Knife." Cited in S. Hanke, ed., *Prospects for Privatization, Proceedings of the Academy of Political Science* 36(3):60-73.

Moore, T. 1970. "The Effectiveness of Regulation of Electric Utility Prices." *Southern Economic Journal* 36:365-75.

Morgan, W. 1977. "Investor Owned vs. Publicly Owned Water Agencies: An Evaluation of the Property Rights Theory of the Firm." *Water Resources Bulletin* 13:775-82.

Morlok, E., and F. Moseley. 1986. "Potential Savings from Competitive Contracting of Bus Transit." Report R-UP9951-86-1, University of Pennsylvania Civil Engineering Department (April).

Morlok, E., and P. Viton. 1985. "The Comparative Costs of Public and Private Providers of Mass Transit." In C. Lave, ed., *Urban Transit*, 233-54. San Francisco: Pacific Institute. Cited in E. Savas, *Privatization: The Key to Better Government.* Chatham, New Jersey: Chatham House.

Mueller, D. 1979. *Public Choice.* Cambridge, U.K.: Cambridge University Press.

Musell, R. 1987. *Contracting Out: Potential for Reducing Federal Costs.* Washington, D.C.: Congressional Budget Office.

Musgrave, R., and P. Musgrave. 1976. *Public Finance in Theory and Practice.* New York: McGraw-Hill.

Muth, F., 1973. *Public Housing: An Economic Evaluation.* Washington, D.C. Cited in T. Borcherding, W. Pommerehne, and F. Schneider, "Comparing the Efficiency of Private and Public Production: The Evidence from Five Countries." *Journal of Economics* (suppl. 2):127-56.

Nelson, R., and S. Winter. 1973. "Toward an Evolutionary Theory of Economic Capabilities." *American Economic Review* 63:440-49 (May).

Neugebauer, G. 1978. *Grundzeuge einer oekonomischen Theories der Korruption.* Zuerich: Schulthess. Cited in T. Borcherding, W. Pommerehne, and F. Schneider, "Comparing the Efficiency of Private and Public Production: The Evidence from Five Countries." *Journal of Economics* (suppl. 2):127-56.

Neustadt, R. 1960. *Presidential Power: The Politics of Leadership.* New York: John Wiley and Sons.

Nicols, A. 1967. "Stock versus Mutual Savings and Loan Associations: Some evidence of Differences in Behavior." *American Economic Review* 57:337-46.

Niskanen, W. 1975. "Bureaucrats and Politicians." *Journal of Law and Economics* 18:617-43 (December).

_____. 1971. *Bureaucracy and Representative Government.* Chicago: Aldine and Atherton.

Noether, M. 1987. *Competition Among Hospitals.* Washington, D.C.: Federal Trade Commission.

Oates, W. 1989. "Searching for Leviathan: A Reply and Some Further Reflections." *American Economic Review* 79(3):578-83 (June).

_____. 1985. "Searching for Leviathan: An Empirical Study." *American Economic Review* 75(4):748-57 (September).

Oelert, W. 1976. "Reprivatisierung des offentlichen Personalverkehrs, wo und wie?" *Der Personenverkehr* 4:108-14. Cited in T. Borcherding, W. Pommerehne, and F. Schneider, "Comparing the Efficiency of Private and Public Production: The Evidence from Five Countries." *Journal of Economics* (suppl. 2):127-56.

Ogur, J., C. Wagner, and M. Vita. 1988. *The Deregulated Airline Industry: A Review of the Evidence.* Washington, D.C.: Federal Trade Commission.

Olson, M. 1965. *The Logic of Collective Action.* Cambridge, Mass.: Harvard University Press.

Palfrey, T., and T. Romer. 1986. "An Experimental Study of Warranty Coverage and Dispute Resolution in Competitive Markets." In P. Ippolito and D. Scheffman, eds., *Empirical Approaches to Consumer Protection Economics.* Washington, D.C.: Federal Trade Commission.

Pausch, R. 1976. *Moglichkeiten einer Privatisierung offentlicher Unternehmen.* Gottingen: Schwartz. Cited in T. Borcherding, W. Pommerehne, and F. Schneider, "Comparing the Efficiency of Private and Public Production: Evidence from Five Countries." *Journal of Economics* (suppl. 2):127-56.

Pautler, P., and M. Vita. 1989. "Hospital Mergers: A Review of the Theory and Evidence." Washington, D.C.: Federal Trade Commission, manuscript.

Pelkmans, J. 1988. "The Internal Markets of North America." Maastricht, Belgium: European Institute of Public Administration (January).

Penn, S. 1988. "New York City Will Confront Mafia in Chinatown By Bidding to Haul Garbage of Some Businesses." *Wall Street Journal* (April 25).

Perloff, J., and M. Wachter. 1984. "Wage Comparability in the U.S. Postal Service." *Industrial and Labor Relations Review* 38(1):26-35 (October).

Perry, J., and T. Babitsky. 1986. "Comparative Performance in Urban Transit: Assessing Privatization Strategies." *Public Administration Review* (January/February):57-66.

Peters, D. 1986. "Success Through Privatization." *Current Municipal Problems* 13:445-51.

Peterson, G. 1981. "Pricing and Privatization of Public Services." Urban Institute Project Report (July).

Peterson, J. 1977. *The Rating Game: Report of the Twentieth Century Fund Task Force on Municipal Bond Credit Ratings.* New York: Twentieth Century Fund.

Petrovic, W., and B. Jaffee. 1977. "Aspects of the Generation and Collection of Household Refuse in Urban Areas." Bloomington: Indiana University. Mimeo. Cited in T. Borcherding, W. Pommerehne, and F. Schneider, "Comparing the Efficiency of Private and Public Production: The Evidecne from Five Countries." *Journal of Economics* (suppl. 2):127-56.

Pfister, W. 1976. "Steigende Millionenverluste der Bayerischen Staatsforstverwaltung: Ein Dauerzustand?" *Mitteilungsblatt des Bayerischen Waldbesitzerverbandes* 2:1-9. Cited in T. Borcherding, W. Pommerehne, and F. Schneider, "Comparing the Efficiency of Private and Public Production: The Evidence from Five Countries." *Journal of Economics* (suppl. 2):127-56.

Pier, W., R. Vernon, and J. Wicks. 1974. "An Empirical Comparison of Government and Private Production Efficiency." *National Tax Journal* 27:653-56.

Pirie, M. 1985. "The British Experience." In S. Butler, ed. *The Privatization Option*, 51-68. Heritage Foundation Lectures #42, Washington, D.C.: Heritage Foundation.

Plott, C. 1982. "Industrial Organization Theory and Experimental Economics." *Journal of Economic Literature* 20(4):1485-1572 (December).

Pommerehne, W., and F. Schneider. 1985. *Private or Public Production: A European Perspective.* Aarhus, Denmark: University of Aarhus.

Pommerehne, W., and B. Frey. 1978. "Bureaucratic Behavior in Democracy." *Public Finance* 33(1-2):98-112. Cited in T. Borcherding, W. Pommerehne, and F. Schneider, "Comparing the Efficiency of Private and Public Production: The Evidence from Five Countries." *Journal of Economics* (suppl. 2):127-56.

_____. 1976. "Private versus offentliche Mullabfuhr; Ein theoretischer und empirischer Vergleich." *Finanzarchiv* 35:272-94. Cited in T. Borcherding, W. Pommerehne, and F. Schneider, "Comparing the Efficiency of Private and Public Production: The Evidence from Five Countries." *Journal of Economics* (suppl. 2):127-56.

Poole, R., Jr. 1983a. "Municipal Services: The Privatization Option." Heritage Foundation Issues Paper No. 238, Washington, D.C.: Heritage Foundation.

_____. 1983b. "Objections to Privatization." *Policy Review* 24:105-19 (Spring).

_____. 1980. *Cutting Back City Hall.* New York: Universe Books.

_____. 1976. "Fighting Fires for Profit." *Reason* 8(1):6-11 (May).

Pound, E., and T. Carrington. 1988. "The Pentagon Mess." *Wall Street Journal* (September 2):1,7.

President's Commission on Privatization. 1988. *Privatization: Toward More Effective Government.* Washington, D.C.: President's Commission on Privatization.

President's Private Sector Survey on Cost Control (Grace Commission). 1983. *President's Private Sector Survey on Cost Control.* Washington, D.C.: President's Private Sector Survey on Cost Control.

Primeaux, W. 1975. "A Reexamination of the Monopoly Market Structure for Electric Utilities." In A. Philips, ed., *Promoting Competition in Regulated Markets*, 175-200. Washington, D.C.: Brookings Institution.

Pryke, R. 1981. *The Nationalized Industries: Policies and Performance Since 1968.* Oxford, U.K.: Martin Robertson.

Putka, G. 1991. "Whittle Develops Plan to Operate Schools for Profit." *Wall Street Journal* (May 15):B1.

Rechnungshof Rheinland-Pfalz. 1972. "Jahresbericht uber die Prufung der Haushalts-und Wirtschaftsfuhrung sowie der Landeshaushaltsrechnung 1971." *Landtags-Drucksache Rheinland-Pfalz* 7/1750:81-84. Cited in T. Borcherding, W. Pommerehne, and F. Schneider, "Comparing the Efficiency of Private and Public Production: Evidence from Five Countries." *Journal of Economics* (suppl. 2):127-56.

Rees, R. 1984. *Public Enterprise Economics.* London: Weidenfield and Nicholson.

Register, C., and E. Bruning. 1987. "Profit Incentives and Technical Efficiency in the Production of Hospital Care." *Southern Economic Journal* 53:899-914.

Rice Center for Urban Mobility Research. 1985. *New Directions in Urban Transportation: Private/Public Partnerships.* Washington, D.C.: U.S. Department of Transportation, Urban Mass Transportation Administration.

Riepma, S. 1970. *The Story of Margarine.* Washington, D.C.: Public Affairs Press.

Robinson, J., and H. Luft. 1988. "Competition, Regulation, and Hospital Costs, 1982-1986." *Journal of the American Medical Association* 260:2676-81.

Rose-Ackerman, S. 1986. *The Economics of Nonprofit Institutions: Studies in Structure and Policy.* New York: Oxford University Press.

Roth, G. 1987. "Airport Privatization." In S. Hanke, ed., *Prospects for Privatization, Proceedings of the Academy of Political Science* 36(3):74-82.

Rudolf, B. 1991. "A Global Fire Sale." *Time* (April 22):58-60.

Savas, E. 1990. "Privatization: A Strategy for Structural Reform." *National Forum: The Phi Kappa Phi Journal* 70(2):9-13 (Spring).

_____. 1987. *Privatization: The Key to Better Government.* Chatham, New Jersey: Chatham House Publishers.

_____. 1981. "Intracity Competition Between Public and Private Service Delivery." *Public Administration Review* 41:46-52 (January/February).

_____. 1980. "Comparative Costs of Public and Private Enterprise." In W. Baumol, ed., *Public and Private Enterprise in a Mixed Economy,* 234-94. New York and London: St. Martin's Press.

_____. 1979. "How Much Do Government Services Really Cost?" *Urban Affairs Quarterly* 15(1):23-42 (September).

_____. 1977a. "An Empirical Study of Competition in Municipal Service Delivery." *Public Administration Review* 37:717-24.

_____. 1977b. *Evaluating the Organization and Efficiency of Solid Waste Collection.* Lexington, Mass.: Lexington Books.

_____. 1974. "Municipal Monopolies vs. Competition in Delivering Urban Services." In W. Hawley and D. Rogers, eds., *Improving the Quality of Urban Management,* 437-500. Beverly Hills, California: Sage Publications.

Scarlett, L. 1988. "Postal Privatization: The Evidence Speaks for Itself." *Privatization Watch* 139:2-3 (June).

Scharfstein, D. 1988. "Product-Market Competition and Managerial Slack." *Rand Journal of Economics* 19(1):147-155 (Spring).

Scherer, F. 1980. *Industrial Market Structure and Economic Performance.* Chicago: Rand McNally.

Schlesinger, M., R. Dorwart, and R. Pulice. 1986. "Competitive Bidding and States' Purchase of Services: The Case of Mental Health Care in Massachusetts." *Journal of Policy Analysis and Management* 5(2):245-63 (1986).

Schmid, R. 1988. "Postal Service Cancels Part of Its Agreement with Perot." *Washington Post* (August 11):E1,E3.

Schneider H., and C. Schuppener. 1971. *Soziale Absicherung der Wohnungs-marktwirtschaft durch Individualsubventionen.* Gottingen: Vandenhoeck and Ruprecht. Cited in T. Borcherding, W. Pommerehne, and F. Schneider, "Comparing the Efficiency of Private and Public Production: Evidence from Five Countries." *Journal of Economics* (suppl. 2):127-56.

Seldon, A. 1982. "Enhancement of Public Sector Efficiency by Micro-Economic Control of Public Supply." In *Public Finance and the Quest for Efficiency, Proceedings of the 38th Congress of the International Instute of Public Finance.* Detroit: Wayne State University Press.

Shapiro, C. 1983. "Premiums for High Quality Products as Returns to Reputation." *Quarterly Journal of Economics* 98:659-679 (November).

Shapiro, C., and R. Willig. 1989. "Privatization to Limit Public-Sector Discretion." Unpublished.

Sharkansky, I. 1975. *Public Administration: Policy Making in Government Agencies.* Chicago: Rand-McNally.

Sherwood, T., and R. Sanchez. 1988. "Barry Shifts Control of Ambulances: City Administrator Replaces Fire Chief as Head of Service." *Washington Post* (February 6):A1, A8, and A9.

Shortell, S., and E. Hughes. 1988. "The Effects of Regulation, Competition, and Ownership on Mortality Rates Among Hospital Inpatients." *New England Journal of Medicine* 318(17):1100-07.

Shulman, M. 1982. "Alternative Approaches for Delivering Public Services." *Urban Data Service Report* 14:10. Washington, D.C.: International City Management Association (October).

Simon, H., D. Smithburg, and V. Thompson. 1950. *Public Administration.* New York: Alfred A. Knopf.

Simon, J., and D. Simon. 1987. "Socialism Verus RPM Versus Free Enterprise: State Liquour Distribution Systems Revisited." Unpublished.

Smith, B. 1987. "The Michigan Accident Fund: A Need for Privatization." Heartland Institute (September 23).

Smith, R. 1983. "Feet to the Fire." *Reason* 14:23-29 (March). Cited in K. Clarkson and P. Fixler, Jr., *The Role of Privatization in Florida's Growth.* Tallahassee, Fl.: Florida Chamber of Commerce Foundation.

Smith, V. 1982. "Competitive Market Institutions: Double Auctions vs Sealed Bid-Offer Auctions." *American Economic Review* 72(1):58-77 (March).

Sonenblum, S., J. Kirlin, and J. Ries. 1977. *How Cities Provide Services: An Evaluation of Alternative Delivery Systems.* Cambridge, Mass.: Ballinger.

Sorkin, A. 1980. *The Economics of the Postal System.* Lexington, Mass.: Lexington Books.

Spann, R. 1977. "Public versus Private Provision of Governmental Services." In T. Borcherding, ed., *Budgets and Bureaucrats: The Sources of Government Growth,* 71-89. Durham, N.C.: Duke University Press.

Stanbury, W. 1987. "Privatization in Canada." Paper delivered at the University of Rochester conference on "Privatization in Britain and North America: Theory, Evidence, and Implementation." Washington, D.C. (November 7).

Starr, P. 1987. "The Limits of Privatization." In S. Hanke, ed., *Prospects for Privatization, Proceedings of the Academy of Political Science* 36(3):124-37.

Stevens, B. 1984. *Delivering Municipal Services Efficiently: A Comparison of Municipal Services Efficiently: A Comparison of Municipal and Private Service Delivery.* Washington, D.C.: U.S. Department of Housing and Urban Development.

Stevens, B., and E. Savas. 1978. "The Cost of Residential Refuse Collection and the Effect of Service Arrangements." *Municipal Year Book* 44:200-205.

Stocker, F. 1973. "Value Determination: The Assessor's Staff vs. the Private Appraisal Firm." In *Property Tax Reform: The Role of the Property Tax in the Nation's Revenue System.* Chicago: International Association of Assessing Officers. Cited in R. Poole, Jr., *Cutting Back City Hall.* New York: Universe Books.

Stolzenberg, R., and S. Berry. 1985. *A Pilot Study of the Impact of OMB Circular A-76 on Motor Vehicle Maintenance Cost and Quality in the U.S. Air Force.* Santa Barbara, California: Rand Corporation.

Talley, W., and E. Anderson. 1986. "Urban Transit Firms Providing Transit, Paratransit, and Contracted-Out Services." *Journal of Transport Economics and Policy* 20(3):353-68 (September).

Taylor, M. 1982. "Volunteerism: A Police Department's Response to Changing Times." *The Police Chief* (May):27-31.

Teal, R. 1986. "Public Transit Service Contracting: A Status Report." Irvine, California: University of California at Irvine, Department of Civil Engineering.

Teal, R., G. Guiliano, and E. Morlok. 1986. "Public Transit Service Contracting." Washington, D.C.: U.S. Urban Mass Transportation Administration (March).

Thompson, V. 1969. *Bureaucracy and Innovation.* University, Alabama: University of Alabama Press.

Thurow, R. 1991. "Seeing the Light." *Wall Street Journal* (September 20):R1-R2.

Tiebout, C. 1956. "A Pure Theory of Local Expenditures." *Journal of Political Economy* 64:416-24.

Tirole, J. 1988. *The Theory of Industrial Organization.* Cambridge, Massachusetts: MIT Press.

Tullock, G. 1965. *The Politics of Bureaucracy.* Washington, D.C.: Public Affairs Books.

Uchitelle, L. 1988. "Public Services Found Better If Private Agencies Compete." *New York Times* (April 26):A1,D18.

U.S. Congressional Budget Office. 1988. *Reducing the Deficit: Spending and Revenue Options*. Washington, D.C.: USGPO.

U.S. Council of Economic Advisors. 1988. *Economic Report of the President, 1988*. Washington, D.C.: USGPO.

_____. 1985. "The Federal Budget and the Economy." In *Economic Report of the President, 1985*, 65-97. Washington, D.C.: USGPO.

U.S. Department of Commerce, Bureau of the Census. 1988. *Government Finances in 1986-87*. Washington, D.C.: USGPO.

_____. 1987. *State Government Finances in 1986*. Washington, D.C.: USGPO.

U.S. Department of Transportation, Urban Mass Transportation Administration. 1985. *New Directions in Urban Transportation: Private/Public Partnerships*. Washington, D.C.: USGPO.

U.S. Federal Trade Commission Staff. 1980. *Handling Consumer Complaints: In-House and Third Party Strategies*. Washington, D.C.: Federal Trade Commission.

U.S. Federal Trade Commission Staff. 1983. "Comments of the FTC Staff, Postal Rate Commission Docket No. R83-1," submitted on June 16.

U.S. General Accounting Office. 1986. *Federal Productivity: Potential Savings from Private Sector Cost Comparisons*. Washington, D.C.: U.S. GAO, December 1986.

_____. 1985a. *Information from Previous Reports on Various Aspects of Contracting Out Under OMB Circular A-76*. Washington, D.C., U.S. GAO (July 5).

_____. 1985b. *DOD Functions Contracted Out Under OMB Circular A-76: Contract Cost Increases and the Effects on Federal Employees*. Washington, D.C.: U.S. GAO (April 15).

_____. 1982a. *Replacing Post Offices With Altenative Services: A Debated But Unresolved Issue*. Washington, D.C.: U.S. GAO (September 2).

_____. 1982b. *The Postal Service Can Substantially Reduce Its Cleaning Costs*. Washington, D.C.: U.S. GAO (December 28).

_____. 1981a. *Review of DOD Contracts Awarded Under OMB Circular A-76*. Washington, D.C.: U.S. GAO (August 26).

_____. 1981b. *GSA's Cleaning Costs Are Needlessly Higher than in the Private Sector*. Washington, D.C.: U.S. GAO (August 24).

_____. 1981c. *Civil Servants and Contract Employees: Who Should Do What for the Federal Government?* Washington, D.C.: U.S. GAO (June 19).

_____. 1981d. *Factors Influencing DOD Decisions to Convert Activities from In-house to Contractor Performance.* Washington, D.C.: U.S. GAO (April 22).

_____. 1978. *Development of a National Make-Or-Buy Strategy -- Progress and Problems.* Washington, D.C.: U.S. GAO (September 12).

U.S. Postal Rate Commission Staff. 1990. *A Study of U.S. Postal Service Productivity and Its Measurement.* Washington, D.C.: U.S. Postal Rate Commission.

U.S. Postal Service. 1987a. *Competitors and Competition for the U.S. Postal Service.* Washington, D.C.: U.S. Postal Service.

_____. 1987b. *Summary Financial and Operating Statements, Accounting Period 12, PFY 1987.* Washington, D.C.: U.S. Postal Service.

Urban Mobility Corp. 1985. *Unsubsidized Transit Services: Potential to Meet Public Needs and Reduce Subsidy Requirements.* Washington, D.C.: U.S. Department of Transportation, Urban Mass Transportation Administration.

Valente, C., and L. Manchester. 1984. *Rethinking Local Services: Examining Alternative Delivery Approaches, Management Information Service Special Report #12.* Washington, D.C.: International City Management Association.

Vickers, J., and G. Yarrow. 1988. *Privatization: An Economic Analysis.* Cambridge, Mass.: MIT Press.

Vita, M., J. Langenfeld, P. Pautler, and L. Miller. 1991. "Economic Analysis in Health Care Antitrust." *The Journal of Contemporary Health Law and Policy* 7(73):73-115.

Wagner, R., and W. Weber. 1975. "Competition, Monopoly, and the Organization of Government in Metropolitan Areas." *Journal of Law and Economics* 18:661-84 (October).

Walberg, H., M. Bakalis, J. Bast, and S. Baer. 1988. *We Can Rescue Our Children.* Chicago: Heartland Institute.

Walker, G., and D. Weber. 1984. "A Transactions Cost Approach to Make-or-Buy Decisions." *Administrative Science Quarterly* 29:373-91.

Walker, M., ed. 1988. *Privatization: Tactics and Techniques.* Vancouver, B.C., Canada: Fraser Institute.

Wallace, R., and P. Junck. 1974. "Implications of Contracting for Public Service." *Urban Affairs Quarterly* 9:337-58.

_____. 1970. "Economic Inefficiency of Small Municipal Electric Generating Systems." *Land Economics* 46:98-104.

Walters, A. 1987. "Ownership and Efficiency in Urban Buses." In S. Hanke, ed., *Prospects for Privatization, Proceedings of the Academy of Political Science* 36(3):83-92.

Wedel, K., A. Katz, and A. Weick, eds. 1979. *Social Services by Government Contract: A Policy Analysis.* New York: Praeger.

Weicher, J. 1980. *Housing.* Washington, D.C.: American Enterprise Institute.

Weisbrod, B. 1977. *The Voluntary Nonprofit Sector.* Lexington, Massachusetts: Lexington Books.

Weiss, L. 1961. *Economics and American Industry.* New York: Wiley and Sons.

Westerhoff, G. 1986. "An Engineer's View of Privatization: The Chandler Experience." *American Waterworks Journal* (February):41-46.

White, L., 1983. *The Public Library in the 1980s: The Problems of Choice.* Lexington, Massachusetts: Lexington Books.

Williams, L. 1988. "Private Post." *Los Angeles Times* (April 25):IV.5.

Williamson, O. 1979. "Transaction-Cost Economics: The Governance of Contractual Relations." *Journal of Law and Economics* 22:233-61 (October).

_____. 1975. *Markets and Hierarchies.* New York: Free Press.

Wilson, G., and J. Jadlow. 1982. "Competition, Profit Incentives, and Technical Efficiency in the Nuclear Medicine Industry." Indiana University, Bloomington. Mimeo. Cited in T. Borcherding, W. Pommerehne, and F. Schneider, "Comparing the Efficiency of Private and Public Production: Evidence from Five Countries." *Journal of Economics* (suppl. 2):127-56.

Wolf, C. 1988. *Markets or Governments: Choosing Between Imperfect Alternatives.* Cambridge, Massachusetts: MIT Press.

World Almanac and Book of Facts, 1988. 1988. New York: Scripps Howard.

Yarrow, G., and J. Vickers. 1987. "Privatization in Theory and Practice in the United Kingdom." Paper delivered at the University of Rochester conference on "Privatization in Britain and North America: Theory, Evidence, and Implementation." Washington, D.C. (November 7).

Yin, R. 1977. "Production Efficiency Versus Bureaucratic Self-Interest: Two Innovative Processes?" *Policy Sciences* 8:381-99.

Yuchtman, E., and S. Seashore. 1971. "A System Resource Approach to Organizational Effectiveness." In J. Maurer, ed., *Readings in Organizational Theory: Open Systems Approaches*, 474-90. New York: Random House.

Zax, J. 1989. "Is There a Leviathan in Your Neighborhood?" *American Economic Review* 79(3):560-67 (June).

Zeckhauser, R., and M. Horn. 1987. "The Principal-Agent Problem and the Management of State-Owned Enterprise." Paper delivered at the

University of Rochester conference on "Privatization in Britain and North America: Theory, Evidence, and Implementation." Washington, D.C. (November 6).

Index

About the Author

JOHN C. HILKE is Staff Economist in the Federal Trade Commission's Bureau of Economics, specializing in issues relating the role of competition to improved economic performance. He is the co-author of *U.S. International Competitiveness: Evolution or Revolution?* (Praeger, 1988).